LEGAL WRITING

WITH STYLE

Terri LeClercq
Senior Lecturer, Legal Writing
University of Texas School of Law

Karin Mika
Professor of Legal Writing
Cleveland-Marshall College of Law

Printed proudly in the United States of America by American workers.

Environmental concerns: Publish-on-demand helps save our trees.

Budget concerns: Publish-on-demand allows students an alternative to expensive text books.

ISBN : 13:978-0692578155
ISBN: 10: 0692578153
LCCN: 2015919963

Dedication

For Jack and the Legal Writing Institute – TLC
To Ralph – KM

Special thanks to my Teaching Assistants, Erick Nevin and Max Julian (Cleveland-Marshall College of Law Class of 2015) without whom this book would not have been completed. Thanks also to Colette Emerson for additional secretarial assistance when most needed, and to Teaching Assistants, Patrick Kramer, and Brittany Lowe (Cleveland-Marshall College of Law Class of 2017). Thanks to Rick Bernet for use of the Harley, and to Debbie Borman for locating the Harley!

Thanks also to our wonderful and supportive colleagues in the extended Legal Writing Community who always leap to helping out both personally and professionally at a moment's notice.

PRAISE for
LEGAL WRITING with STYLE

"Why do students enter law school? To learn how to be lawyers. Lawyers write. This book reviews basics and teaches legal style, so students are prepared to write when they leave us. **What's not to like?**"
Shelley Broderick, Dean, University of District of Columbia Law School

"A **modern-day *Elements of Style* for law students** ... perfect complement to any basic legal writing course book."
Nancy A. Wanderer, University of Maine School of Law

"This compact text is designed for first-year law students, but practicing attorneys will benefit from this excellent review of basics and legal style. I especially appreciate the **constant reminder that we must remember ethical communication--the cornerstone of legal practice**."
Broadus Spivey, Spivey & Grigg, LLP, Former president State Bar of Texas

"Short, affordable, and full of great advice … **an abundance of examples** will appeal to legal writers of all levels."
Lurene Contento, The John Marshall Law School

"If you believe the journey to persuasive legal writing begins at Density Drive, circles Pretention Plaza and arrives at Arcane Avenue, then you will neither enjoy nor benefit from this book."
Bobby Hawthorne, author of award-winning <u>Radical Write!!</u>

"If you're ready to take your legal writing to the next level, then this short and sassy exploration of the style, ethics, and strategies that are the **hallmark of truly readable and elegant legal writing** is for you."
Ruth Ann McKinney, UNC School of Law, author of <u>Core Grammar</u>

"… **perfect for a legal writing class**… focuses on the stylistic and grammatical issues with which law students are most likely to struggle… short exercises throughout reinforce the classroom or allow students to complete at home."
Kamina Pender, Mercer University School of Law

"Law students with science and math backgrounds may wonder if their grasp of basic sentence structure is good enough for legal documents. This book's instruction, examples, and exercises will take them on the path to clear, concise legal writing. It is a **must-have for students and lawyers alike**."

Wendy Wagner, University of Texas, author of award-winning <u>Bending Science</u>

"This book's **distinction between undergraduate papers and legal memos guides novice students** through the many unique requirements of legal writing."

Cathren Page Koehlert, Barry School of Law

"Professors LeClercq and Mika zero in on the exact issues that cause lawyers problems and then provide clear solutions. **This little book will become your trusty, dog-eared legal writing companion."**

Tracy McGaugh Norton, Touro Law Center, author of <u>Interactive Citation Workbook</u>

"All lawyers write; successful lawyers are those who write well ... a helpful resource for lawyers who want to refresh their writing or to improve the writing of those they supervise... the exercises that accompany each topic provide essential practice for identifying and correcting writing problems. **Buy this book; you actually will use it**."

Sam Jacobson, Willamette Law School, author of <u>Legal Analysis and Communication</u>

"An easy-to-use reference for writers of all ilk, *Legal Writing with Style* **succinctly answers those pesky writing questions that plague us all**. For law students and legal writing faculty, the book is a boon. A quick look at *Legal Writing with Style* will help students and practitioners avoid those writing mistakes and miscues that drive faculty and judges to distraction."

Jeanne Price, University of Nevada Las Vegas

"This book is a gem. If you are a legal professional looking to improve your own writing skills, start here. If you are a law professor searching for practical pointers to polish your students' writing skills, stop your search here. **No book accomplishes more with fewer words or a better sense of humor.**"

Walter Wright, Texas State University

"For lawyers and students, this book is **short, witty, and easy to use**."

Richard K. Neumann, Hofstra Law School, author of <u>Essential Lawyering Skills</u>

LEARNING THE LAW IS TOUGH ENOUGH; LEARNING TO WRITE ABOUT THE LAW? EVEN TOUGHER. YOU NEED TO MASTER THE BASICS, AND YOU NEED **STYLE**!

style

Who/Did/What/To Whom?

Who-Did-What-to Whom?

WHO-DID-WHAT-TO-WHOM?

Who-Did-
What-to-
Whom?

Style

SUMMARY OF CONTENTS

TABLE OF CONTENTS

Over 1 million happy
people severed in 2015!
Fry Palace
356 W 5th St.
Chicago, Ill 60605

MESSAGE TO STUDENTS

So here you are in law school, and it's back to learning how to write.

Why study writing – again?

No matter what academic and life experiences you've already had, you will immediately realize that legal writing is different. Writing for legal audiences is a skill, and, like any new skill, it has to be practiced.
Yes, it's still writing, but it is a **branch** of technical writing with its own set of rules and priorities. Although you learned to write in grade school, composed essays and organized reports in high school, and perhaps created analytic discussions in college or on the job, there's more! Each of those writing stages helped you reach the next stage – and then the next stage.

Now you've reached a narrowed branch within a very specific field of technical writing. It is nothing like the writing you have done before, and yet requires the application of all of the skills you've learned. Once you've learned how to employ the skills you've already learned, you will unlock an entirely new world of communication.

When learning this form of writing, you will also discover that it reflects the very skills you will learn in all of your law classes: spotting legal issues, deriving rules (both broad rules and narrow rules) comparing (as well as) contrasting cases, and applying rules to unique fact situations. When you begin writing legal documents for class, your first attempts will follow the outline your writing professor provides, and you may, at first become frustrated by the restrictions on your creativity and personal style. Is written legal analysis formulaic? Yes. So was learning the four-paragraph essay. Novice writers have to know the general skeleton required before they can leap off into a research paper; so, too, you need to practice the basic outlines for legal writing.

Legal writing is demanding in ways that undergraduate writing rarely is, perhaps because legal writing requires you to understand the law with so much depth that you will be able to recognize both sides of any issue and strategize about possible ways to benefit your client while remaining ethical in terms of how adverse law is explained and portrayed to all of your readers. So, while you are absorbing an incredible amount of substance, you must also be paring it down to its most precise and concise written form so that it is easily understood for your audience. It is quite a task to attempt master, and, frankly, takes a lifetime of practice and continuous honing to truly be an expert.

Why should I spend so much time on writing when I need to spend time learning the material in my other classes?

Many students enter law school believing that legal studies will be all about substance. This couldn't be further from the truth. The study of law does require being immersed in legal substance, but the practice of law requires that an attorney be able to communicate legal analysis clearly – and most often, in writing. The challenge of combining brand new concepts with a brand new methodology of thought and into clearly articulated writing is daunting for even the best writers.

Your legal writing class will offer concrete feedback about organizing, analyzing, and applying law to facts. Take seriously your instruction. Your writing will become the bread and butter of your profession.

Practicing legal writing is practicing the law. Learning to be concise is learning to focus on the essential issues and cut out extraneous material. Learning to find the precise precedent and precise word is learning to analyze within your writing.

Visualize an audience of hurried, irritated, and probably bored readers. You must convince them that you have something you need them to read – something that is beneficial for them, and something that is worth their time. Whatever you are writing might be important to you, but it is not necessarily as important to the reader.

Remember, too, that attorneys and judges often spend all day reading (as you will when you are an attorney). Few people want to spend their time trying to wade their way through convoluted and confusing writing. If a person is forced into trying to decipher difficult text, the first inclination of the person is not to want to bother. You definitely do not want a judge, boss, or professor not to want to bother reading what you might have written. Your career will depend on others bothering to read what you have written.

Keep in mind that the writing experience of law school will probably be much different than the writing experience in undergraduate school. In undergraduate school, it is rare that professors have the luxury of being able to comment on both substance and precision of wording; thus students often get sloppy. Drafts and papers are often done the night before they are due, and students rarely learn the process of perfecting one's work. The law school, experience, however, will be much different.

If legal writing is so different than the type of writing done in undergraduate school, why are the casebooks filled with convoluted opinions?

Not many readers can defend the prose of some of the judicial opinions selected for casebooks. However, many novice law students are convinced that this is the way communicating legally looks and sound. We can't really defend the prose, but we can attempt to explain it so that you understand why the prose shouldn't be emulated:

- Many of the cases were written years ago when writers used a more lofty, elevated language;
- the casebook authors include cases based on the issues presented and not because they are well written; and
- there are a lot of poor writers in the legal profession.

Don't join the poor writers yourself. Remember your frustration when you read your casebooks or any other convoluted prose. You don't want your readers to respond that way to your own prose.

HOW TO MAKE THE BEST USE OF THE BOOK

The book is meant to be a purely practical guide to the expectations of writing like a lawyer. The book is divided into six parts that can help you break down the task of editing your drafts into credible final products. First review the basic rules of professional writing by trying the two exercises in Chapter 1. Once you're assured that you remember the rules required for professional writing, then use the remainder of this book to help hone your writing skills. Here are a few helpful checklists:

CHECKLIST for SENTENCES, Chapter 2:

- Are my sentences short enough?
- Have I placed my verb close to its subject?
- Is the main clause clear in relation to the dependent clause?
- Are modifiers close to the noun they modify?
- Did I add signposts in longer sentences?
- Did I dovetail thoughts to help sentence coherency?
- Did I examine modifier placement?
- Are parallel ideas represented by parallel structure?
- Did I examine whether the use of passive construction was appropriate?
- Did I place citations appropriately to ensure sentences flow?
- Are long quotations necessary, or is it better to paraphrase them?

CHECKLIST for WORDS, Chapter 3:

- Have I edited to eliminate legal jargon?
- Have I maintained a professional tone?
- Did I edit to create strong nouns and verbs?
- Did I delete unnecessary words?
- Did I edit to replace nominalizations?
- Did I review my list of frequently misused words?

CHECKLIST for PUNCTUATION, Chapter 4:

- Do my punctuation marks help the reader to understand the substantive material?
- Have I used punctuation marks correctly?
- Have I double-checked those marks required specifically for legal writers?
- Have I double-checked plurals and possessives to ensure my apostrophes are used correctly?

CHECKLIST for ORGANIZATION, Chapter 5:

- Did I conscientiously shift from undergraduate to legal organization?
- Can readers easily find both the conclusion and setup at the beginning of my document?
- Do my headings and topic sentences reflect the order of the setup?
- Can readers follow the coherent whole through my use of carefully chosen transitions?

CHECKLIST for PRESENTATION, Chapter 6:

- Is my document visually inviting?
- Is the organization readily apparent?
- Can readers understand what is important through my use of alignment, white space, font, and paragraph/sentence length?
- Have I proofread my document?

This book cannot answer all of your style questions or calm all of your anxieties. But if you use it as a springboard for constant and deliberate practice, you'll develop the professional style of a careful legal writer.

Terri LeClercq and Karin Mika 2015

♦ ♦ ♦ ♦

Good writers are those who keep the language efficient. That is to say, keep it accurate, keep it clear.

EZRA POUND

♦ ♦ ♦ ♦

1 REVIEWING THE BASICS

Credibility, credibility, credibility. Those are three answers to your first question. "Why review basics—again?"

Here's why: if you can't grasp the basic rules of Standard English, no one will believe you can grasp the fine points of a legal argument. This short introductory chapter offers you a chance to double-check your Standard-English skills: can you edit a sentence that has a grammar error? an incorrect punctuation mark? a misused word? Let's see.

Below is a Basic Review Quiz that highlights clear, understandable English. The answers follow immediately. If you ace that one (or even if you don't), then move on to the Higher Competency Quiz, which is slightly more challenging. The answers to it are in the Appendix.

If taking these quizzes reveals that you've forgotten a few of the finer points, or that you were never taught some of these rules, then this book will help clear up those problems while introducing stylistic difference and requirements of legal writing.

BASIC REVIEW

1. The lead counsel, in addition to her office administrator and paralegals, are bringing in exhibits in cardboard boxes.

2. Court personnel judge you by your clothing and your grooming irregardless of any published standards.

3. After cutting through the technical jargon and massive sets of exhibits, a decision was reached in two days.

4. The defendants briefing relied on *ad hominem* attacks that were not relevant or helpful to the court's resolution.

5. We vacate the portion of the district court's order that finalizes the fee award and reducing the total fee.

6. Plaintiff lawyers looked at each other and at the floor; they had not expected this.

7. They had tried to insure their success with the volume of exhibits.

8. Each of the lawyers tried not to let their disappointment show to their client.

9. As the courtroom cleared, the lawyers and paralegals picked up their materials, slowly they joined their client.

10. The client was sitting in the first row, and was confused.

ANSWERS TO BASIC REVIEW

1. Subject/verb agreement. The main subject is "lead counsel," singular; the verb needs to match: lead counsel **is**.

2. Word choice. "Irregardless" is not standard English, so replace it with "regardless": grooming **regardless** of.

3. Dangling element. "After cutting" is a modifier that requires a logical antecedent; it's not the decision doing that cutting. So either:

(1) **After the jury** cut through the technical jargon and massive sets of exhibits, a *decision* was reached in two days. *Or*,

(2) After cutting through the technical jargon and massive sets of exhibits, **the jury** reached a decision in two days.

4. Punctuation possessive. It is the briefing of the defendant(s) and thus requires possessive case. So either:

(1) if more than one defendant, "The defendant**s'** briefing relied . . . ." *or*,

(2) if only one defendant, "The defendant**'s** briefing relied . . . ."

5. Parallelism (equal parts of the sentence require equal grammatical forms). The verbs "finalizes" and "reducing" both follow "that" and should be grammatically parallel and equal. Thus: that **finalizes** the fee award and **reduces** the total fee.

6. Ambiguous pronoun. The demonstrative pronoun "this" needs an antecedent. For example: They had not expected the court **to vacate or to reduce the awards.**

7. Incorrect word. "Insure" applies to insurance and money; "ensure" is to make certain or safe. Thus: tried **to ensure** their success.

8. Pronoun consistency. "Each" is singular and means "each one." The subsequent pronouns need to be singular also; an alternative is to replace the "each" with a plural concrete noun ("the lawyers") or a plural pronoun ("they"). Rather than mixing singular and plural, you have three options:

(1) "**Each** tried not to let **his or her** disappointment . . ."

(2) "The **lawyers** tried not to let **their** disappointment show," *or*

(3) "**They** tried not to let . . ." (although "they" may be ambiguous if the sentence contains other plural nouns).

9. Comma splice. "[S]lowly they joined their client" is an independent clause. Two independent clauses require stronger connections than the comma. The sentence may be corrected in several ways:

(1) a semicolon: "materials**; s**lowly, they," *or*

(2) a period: "materials**. S**lowly they," *or*

(3) a comma joined by a conjunction: "materials**, and** slowly . . ."

10. Separation of subject and its verb by an unnecessary comma. Although subjects can be separated from their verbs by two commas for interrupters (the students, who were unhappy, continued), subjects cannot be sliced away from their verbs by only one comma. Thus: first **row and was confused.**

OK, now you've tested yourself. How did you do? These samples reflect the pitfalls that destroy credibility, and you simply can't afford to sign a document containing them. So maybe, if you didn't score as high as you thought you would, you can improve the score on the exercise below. Perhaps you were just getting warmed up. Try again; the answers are in the Appendix.

HIGHER COMPETENCY QUIZ

The answers to the Higher Competency Quiz can be found on page 95.

1. Mr. Helm, seeking to overturn his sentence, sued the state, saying it violated the 18th Amendment's prohibition against "cruel and unusual punishment" with the no-parole add-on to his life sentence, and failing to apply any proportionality test.

2. "Prison for life" is different than "prison for life without parole."

3. He asked his attorneys to "please send the history of earlier cases to my wife and myself" so the two could help the team with the research.

4. All the cases and the anecdotes over 10-years-old were not helpful.

5. Attorneys acknowledged that Helm had a fraudulent check for $100 that was cashed at the grocery store.

6. Since Helm had been arrested for three drunk-driving offenses, the system had already labeled him as a recidivist.

7. One question was whether this history was only for "relatively 'minor' crimes."

8. The court looked at three objective criteria which it enumerated in the opinion for the first time.

9. Mr. Helm had a great deal at stake, he had quit drinking and had made a mistake with the check.

10. In 1995, the Supreme Court narrowed the earlier proportionality guarantee principle with five more principles to use in cases of life without parole.

After grading yourself on both these exercises, you may be relieved that your past grammar practice has provided a strong background, and you can turn cheerfully to the next chapter. You might, though, have a few misgivings and decide you need a bit more practice as you write that first memo. You may even be dismayed because you missed quite a few of the answers. Everyone has areas of strengths and weaknesses; if the basics of grammar and punctuation are a weakness, do take every opportunity to practice. Good luck!

Karin is astounded by the preposition she has just been presented.

♦♦♦♦

There are only two cures for the long sentence: (1) Say less; (2) Put a period in the middle. Neither expedient has taken hold in the law.

DAVID MELLINKOFF, THE LANGUAGE OF THE LAW 366 (1963).

♦♦♦♦

2 CREATING SENTENCES WITH STYLE

Let's focus on your sentence style. In undergraduate writing, your sentences evolved fairly naturally out of your ideas and research. As you have already seen from casebooks, legal writing doesn't look like it "evolved fairly naturally." Au contraire. Legal opinions, especially those opinions studied early in the first year, look as though they were written specifically to exhaust readers in their efforts to learn about what's going on. Fortunately, your job is not to write those types of opinions. Unfortunately, by the time you receive your first law school writing assignment, you've already been subliminally tainted by case law and its convolutions. Thus, you may be tempted to go out and write likewise. Don't.

Your writing professors will be emphasizing over and over again that writing is a process. Once law students master the concept of legal analysis, they must make sure that whatever documents they ultimately produce is well-organized and written in language that is clear and easily understood. This process does not conclude in a few hours but often takes days, weeks, or even months (depending on complexity of project). It takes careful reading, re-reading, and tinkering with the nuances of language.

Assume for a minute that you have already created a draft. Set that draft aside for a while and spend a little time working on the material for your other classes. Your other professors will be quite appreciative. Then, before turning in whatever writing assignment you're working on, go back to the draft and focus on readability: will your readers understand everything on a first read-through, or are your sentences so long and convoluted that your readers will be forced either to reread or to abandon all hope?

Predictably and sadly, it takes most new law students only about a week before they begin producing sentences that resemble those in casebooks. That's natural, but counterproductive.

This chapter examines problems that commonly affect the readability of sentence-level prose: sentences that are simply tough to read; sentences with errors that create ambiguity; and sentences with case names and citations that boggle normal syntax. One technique for reviewing your draft is to look at the individual sentences and ask: Who Did What to Whom? Or, What did I mean to say about what? You can edit many weak sentences into powerful ones by adding an "actor" into sentences that originally were passive. You can also improve sentences by cutting down the length, or giving the reader more cues about what's happening. The idea behind this review of sentence structure is that you'll return to your draft and tackle each sentence until it says specifically and concretely what you want it to say. That requires time—the same sort of time your future legal documents will demand.

1. Creating and Connecting Clear Sentences with Style

- Long sentences
- Subject/verb separation
- Front-loaded sentences
- Missing signposts
- Dovetailing and repetition
- Passive/active voices

2. Avoiding Error

- Modifier placement, proximity
- Modifier placement, ambiguity
- Dangling elements
- That/which
- Faulty parallelism
- Multiple pronoun antecedents
- Antecedents of demonstrative and relative pronouns
- Ambiguous noun and pronoun substitutes

3. Incorporating Authority

- Awkward citation placement
- Excessive/intrusive quotations

CREATING AND CONNECTING CLEAR SENTENCES WITH STYLE

Most legal sentences are too long and too convoluted for easy reading. You will find copious examples the first time you open any casebook to a random page. Those long sentences are the result of legal training that, as you are learning, is a process of qualifying, narrowing, and delineating with evidence. Thus, your new skill at qualifying and delineating while you are "thinking like a lawyer" can inadvertently result in a chain of clauses that become long, convoluted written sentences. One frustrating and "tough" aspect of legal sentences is their unending dependent clauses. These clauses are, perhaps, first formulated in the classroom when you attempt to answer a professor's pounding questions. You qualify simple, declarative sentences with independent, qualifying phrases. That qualification helps with classroom answers, certainly, but wreaks havoc on the clarity of your writing.

Not all long sentences are difficult reading, of course; many a long sentence has been written with perfect clarity. If legal sentences are carefully punctuated and cued, then necessary qualifying clauses will not affect their readability. Without proper cueing, though, a chain of embedded, dependent clauses will confuse readers.

Let's look at an example:

In *Richert*, the estate of the nursing home resident, who had been diagnosed with dementia and who suffered fatal injuries after falling from the roof of the facility despite numerous warnings to the nursing home personnel that the patient tended to wander unsupervised to the roof, sued a county nursing home for negligence and wrongful death alleging state as well as federal nursing home residents' rights violations, seeking compensatory and punitive damages for the injuries of the deceased as well as damages for the mental anguish of the survivors.If your consciousness began drifting away as you tried to follow that prose, you are not alone. Now, try to imagine your professor grading 30, 40, or more papers that are filled with long, convoluted sentences. That professor will not be a very happy person, and she will be less likely to appropriately reward brilliance when she sees it.

SOLUTIONS

Let's take our *Richert* sentence from above as an example. If we follow some simple guidelines, we can translate the story into something that can be more easily understood. We will also have a checklist for simplifying any type of lengthy and convoluted sentence, or series of convoluted sentences.

1. Where possible, **break long sentences** down into multiple sentences. Limit each shortened sentence to one or two main ideas. **Insert sentence subjects** where necessary.

☑ In *Richert*, the estate of a nursing home resident sued a county nursing home for negligence and wrongful death. **The patient** had been diagnosed with dementia and had suffered fatal injuries after falling from the roof of the facility. **Nursing home personnel had been warned** that the patient tended to wander unsupervised to the roof. **The plaintiff's estate** alleged state as well as federal nursing home residents' rights violations. **The plaintiff** sought compensatory and punitive damages for the injuries of the deceased as well as damages for the mental anguish of the survivors.

*Note also that when you break down a lengthy sentence, your verbs will sometimes have to be modified to make sure that the sentences remain logical.

2. **Place the subject close to the verb** and place both of them toward the beginning of the sentence.

Let's take a look at our lengthy sentence again. If we closely examine the sentence, we know that the main theme of the sentence is that the **estate** of the deceased **sued** the nursing home. However, with all of that additional descriptive information thrown in, that main idea becomes lost. However (as demonstrated by the revised example from above), if we place the main subject close to the main verb, readers can find that main focus:

☑ In *Richert*, **the estate** of a nursing home resident **sued** a county nursing home for negligence and wrongful death.

The same clarity is demonstrated below by the remaining sentences in what has now become a paragraph. When the subject is placed close to the verb, the meaning of each sentence is clear:

- ☑ **The patient had been diagnosed** with dementia and **had suffered fatal injuries** after falling from the roof of the facility.
- ☑ **Nursing home personnel had been warned** that the patient tended to wander unsupervised to the roof.
- ☑ **The plaintiff alleged** state as well as federal nursing home residents' rights violations.
- ☑ **The plaintiff sought** compensatory and punitive damages for the injuries of the deceased as well as damages for the mental anguish of the survivors.

3. **Revise front-loaded sentences.** Make sure that your main ideas are placed at the beginnings of a sentence, and that they are not hidden after a long, descriptive "front-loaded" dependent clause.

Introductory dependent clauses—those that appear at the beginning of a sentence and are set off by a comma—may provide information that is not necessarily essential to the main theme. When introductory dependent clauses are lengthy, they can cause the same type of mental glazing over that lengthy sentences can cause. The reader simply can't hold all that introductory language in abeyance until the main noun shows up.

Here's an example:

Convicted of each of the 31 counts that ranged from mail fraud to fraudulently procuring government contracts (except for one count of obstructing justice brought against only one of the defendants) and convinced that their conduct was within the range acceptable for government employees, the **defendants**, who filed separately and collectively in several different courts, **appealed** their convictions.

This sentence places over 40 words *before* the beginning of the main clause—and the main subject (the defendants) is then separated by ten more words from the sentence's active verb (appealed).

Several techniques can help improve clarity in front-loaded sentences.

a. **Break apart** a front-loaded sentence into multiple sentences and eliminate unnecessary descriptive language. Use transitions where necessary:

The **defendants were convicted** of each of the 31 counts, except one defendant who was not convicted of obstructing justice. The **defendants were convinced** that their conduct was within the range acceptable for government employees. Therefore, the **defendants appealed** their convictions separately and collectively.

b. **Break up** front-loaded sentences by **flip-flopping** the ideas so that the main subject and verb are first:

The **defendants appealed** their convictions both separately and collectively on the basis that they believed that their conduct was within the range acceptable for government employees. These **appeals followed** convictions on each of the 31-count indictments, except for the acquittal of one defendant on the charge of obstructing justice.

Note that in each of the revised examples above, some of the detail is left out. When drafting first assignments, first-year students tend to include all kinds of detail because they simply do not know what is important and what may be left out. The task becomes even more difficult because what is important may change depending on the task.

For instance, in our sentence above, is it really that important that there were 31 counts to the indictment and that only one defendant was charged with, and acquitted of, obstructing justice? Is the range of charges important? Does it matter why the defendants believed that they were unfairly convicted or that they appealed both collectively and separately?

The answer to any one of these questions might be that the information is indeed important; however, it is the writer's obligation to determine what information is important and then to edit as necessary.

c. Eliminate extraneous detail not necessary to the task. By axing the unnecessary detail, we might even be able to distill our front-loaded sentence into something quite simple:

- Convicted of most of the counts in the indictment, the defendants appealed; *or*,
- Believing that their conduct was acceptable, the defendants appealed their convictions.

Consider also this bit of strategy: you may deliberately create a front-loaded sentence if you would like to downplay some information. This deliberate placement is a stylistic technique sophisticated writers use when they would like the court to focus on favorable facts as opposed to unfavorable facts.

Here are a few examples:

- Although the company had been fined previously, the court viewed the oil spill as an unforeseeable accident. (downplaying the earlier fine)
- Even though the singer was not known for her warm and fuzzy nature, there was no indication that she was a poor parent. (downplaying the singer's less-than-affectionate personality trait)

4. Add word and punctuation signposts if the sentence length is absolutely necessary (or at least absolutely desired).

When reading court opinions or examining samples of legal memos, you might notice that long sentences are encouraged or even expected as part of appropriate legal analysis. For instance, issue statements and statements of position often include numerous "legal" components such as the parties, the cause of action, the status of the court proceedings, a statute or other law that might be at issue, and any relevant facts related to the cause of action.

For example, a typical issue statement might look like this:

Whether the Court of Appeals was correct when it determined that the defendant's Fifth Amendment right to counsel was not violated when the defendant had requested an attorney but was still questioned by police officers after he was placed in a holding cell.

Generally, however, first-year students do not arrive at law school having the knack of writing coherent lengthy "legal" sentences. Thus, first-year law students tend to mesh all kinds of concepts together, whether in issue statements or in other sentences.

Here's an example:

The court held that the murder convictions were based on insufficient evidence to support a charge of premeditated murder, that the jury instruction for manslaughter should have been given, and that the testimony of the government's psychological expert should have been excluded, remanding the case to the lower court for a new trial.

Careful **word signposting** can help clarify purposely long sentences by signaling relationships: transitions, repetitions of words or phrases, introductions, and conclusions:

The court **first** held that the murder convictions were based on insufficient evidence to support a charge of premeditated murder, **then determined** that the jury instruction for manslaughter should have been given, and **finally concluded** that the testimony of the government's psychological expert should have been excluded **before** remanding the case to the lower court for a new trial.

In addition to word signposts, **punctuation signposts** can make the message more accessible, as the following colon illustrates:

On appeal, the defendant's attorney had one primary **argument: that** the confession should have been excluded because it violated the defendant's Fifth Amendment right to counsel.

Finally, if a sentence contains numerous components that are particularly unwieldy but necessary, you can also use **numbered lists (tabulation) and appropriate transitions** to create an organizational hierarchy (and add white space to the page).

Compare:

The Dog Bite statute sets out that an owner of a dog may be strictly liable for the dog's biting an individual when the owner knew that the dog had vicious propensities, or if the dog had previously acted aggressively although unprovoked, or if the dog had been encouraged to engage in aggressive behavior by the owner, but provides a defense to the owner if it can be demonstrated that there were circumstances beyond anyone's control that caused the dog to become aggressive.

With:

The Dog Bite statute sets out that an owner of a dog may be strictly liable for the dog's biting an individual **under the following circumstances**:

1. when the owner knew that the dog had vicious propensities, or
2. if the dog had previously acted aggressively although unprovoked, or
3. if the dog had been encouraged to engage in aggressive behavior by the owner.

However, the statute provides a defense to the owner if it can be demonstrated that there were circumstances beyond anyone's control that caused the dog to become aggressive.

Now that we've examined ways to improve lengthy sentences, let's focus on improving sentences in general. Recall that the object of legal style is to be as clear and precise in as few words as possible. Because many of the topics you will be writing about are not innately clear and precise, you will be required to do a fair amount of translating of the material into something that the reader can easily understand. Here are a few tips for improving how you convey your legal knowledge:

5. **Dovetailing and repetition** can link thoughts together and give the reader context[1].

Dovetailing is a device used to link the main ideas of sentences together so that the reader has context for the material being read. Dovetailing also adds a nice narrative fluidity to your work. Dovetailing is important in legal writing both because the material tends to be complex (the reader needs to be reminded Who Did What to Whom) and because

[1] Dovetailing is also discussed in Chapter Five, Organizing with Style.

legal writing always involves various components of cases that have been decided at various levels of courts. However, dovetailing sentences in legal writing is not always sufficient in making a sequence clear. You can also experiment with **repetition** (repeating words or phrases) to link ideas and emphasize them.

Let's examine this sequence:

In *Lurep Industries v. Indigo Yarn*, the court held that the plaintiff was not entitled to damages after it was sold an inadequately colored batch of yarn. The plaintiff traditionally ordered a specific shade of blue yarn for its sweaters. A bad batch of yarn caused the company to produce sweaters that were not up to standards. The error was not discovered until after the sweaters were manufactured and resulted in a loss of $100,000. The lower court found the company was entitled to damages. The court of appeals determined that the yarn was not examined in a timely fashion. There were also other options to purchase the same shade of yarn from other suppliers. The ruling was reversed.

If the first question on your mind is, "What? Who actually won the case?" then you've picked up on the problem. We've got two court decisions here, and the paragraph is not clear as to the relationship between the facts, the cause of action, and what the lower court and appellate court decided. You can clear up this confusion with a few modifications:

In *Lurep Industries v. Indigo Yarn*, the **court of appeals held** that the plaintiff was not entitled to damages after being sold an inadequately colored batch of yarn. ***Lurep*** **involved a company** that had traditionally ordered a specific shade of blue yarn for its sweaters. **The company** received a bad batch of yarn that caused the company to produce sweaters that were not up to standards. The company did not discover the error until after the sweaters were manufactured, **and as a result, the company** lost $100,000. **In finding that the lower court erred in awarding damages, the court of appeals reasoned** that **the company** did not examine the yarn in a timely fashion. **The court further reasoned** that there were also other options **for the company** to purchase the same shade of yarn from other suppliers.

6. In general, your writing will be more understandable if you write in **active**, rather than passive, **voice.**

A verb is "active" when the subject of the sentence is performing the action: "The **court held** that the defendant was negligent." But if the subject is acted upon by something else (as this very clause demonstrates), the verb is passive. *The plaintiff was injured by the vehicle*.

Let's take a look at this sequence:

In *Morris*, a ruling was made by the court in which it was decided that a wrongful discharge cause of action had been appropriately brought by the plaintiff who had been fired. An allegation was made that a wrongful request had been made by the employer in which illegal manipulation of financial records had been done by the employee at the request of the employer. This manipulation was reported by the employee to the Federal Trade Commission, and the employment of the plaintiff was terminated.

A little bit difficult to wade through? That's because the sequence is written almost entirely in the passive voice. [Don't confuse the passive voice with the past tense: *The attorney had defended and prosecuted the same man*. (past tense but active voice)]

Overuse or inadvertent use of the passive voice causes several problems:

a. The passive voice adds unnecessary words.

In *Morris*, a ruling was made by the court in which it was decided that a wrongful discharge cause of action had been appropriately brought by the plaintiff who had been fired. (32 words)

In *Morris*, the **court ruled** that the **plaintiff proved** his wrongful discharge cause of action. (15 words)

An allegation was made that a wrongful request had been made by the employer in which illegal manipulation of financial records had been done by the employee at the request of the employer. (33 words)

The **employee alleged** that his **employer asked** him to illegally manipulate financial records. (13 words)

This manipulation was reported by the employee to the Federal Trade Commission, and the employment of the plaintiff was terminated. (20 words; who terminated him?)

The **employee reported** the manipulation to the Federal Trade Commission, and **his employer** then terminated him. (16 words)

b. The passive voice steals the punch from strong, active verbs.

The plaintiff was injured by the defendant.

The defendant **injured** the plaintiff.

c. The passive voice introduces ambiguity: "truncated" passives (person/agent missing).

No **rebuttal was made** regarding allegations of employee theft. (who might have rebutted?)

The Union **did not rebut** allegations of employee theft.

On the other hand, the passive voice is occasionally useful when used deliberately:

- when you *do not know* the agent/actor.

  The girl was propelled out of the train.

- when you need to *protect* your agent/actor from a direct accusation.

  Marta was dismissed from law school.

- when you want to *emphasize the result* of an action.

  George was murdered by a drunken driver.

Overall, the passive voice, when used intelligently, can be a useful tool for providing the appropriate clarity and emphasis in your writing.

Try These

EXERCISE 1. CREATING AND CONNECTING CLEAR SENTENCES WITH STYLE

The answers to Exercise 1 can be found on page 96.

Revise the following difficult sentences so that their ideas are conveyed more clearly—divide into several sentences, add transitions, move elements, etc. Explain what style problem(s) created any confusion.

1. The district court, noting that the expert witness had no qualifications to be testifying about the physics of rocket fuel, and further noting that the flashpoint of the rocket fuel was irrelevant in relation to the action for battery, concluded that the testimony should not have been admitted.

2. The judge, having already revealed going to high school with the plaintiff's attorney and having children who went to the same school as the plaintiff, recused himself from the case.

Experiment with flip-flopping and then breaking apart these sentences. Work on placing subjects close to their verbs and on appropriately connecting your material. Explain the problems.

3. If the prosecution suppresses requested evidence favorable to an accused when the evidence is material either to guilt or punishment, irrespective of the good or bad faith of the prosecution, this suppression may violate due process.

4. The Chief Justice, who was writing on behalf of a majority of Justices who determined that the search was unconstitutional, wrote that the confession should have been suppressed because the defendant had requested counsel when he was first placed in the police car, had repeated his request while in a holding cell, and had only confessed when told that his attorney would be delayed by a few hours.

Practice the art of dovetailing these sentences.

5. Two of the judges questioned the procedural problem with the case. The attorney had mislabeled the Motion.

6. The plaintiff's allegation was that she was a victim of intentional infliction of emotional distress. A plaintiff must prove that the defendant engaged in behavior that is purposely malicious and goes "beyond the decency of the norms of a polite society."

Switch the following passive constructions into the active voice. (Add or change words for clarity where necessary.)

7. A nationally syndicated columnist was plagiarized in a law-student newsletter by a third-year student.

8. The plagiarism was uncovered by the Federalist Society.

AVOIDING SENTENCE ERRORS

In addition to unraveling "tough" sentences and sentence connections, new legal writers need to concentrate on tough sentences that contain actual errors. Let's assume you know a basic grammar or punctuating error when you see it. Now you're practicing the fine art of balancing heavy, new legal concepts with the need to qualify and modify your ideas; that balance is going to be a challenge to your grasp of basic grammar. You don't want to confuse readers right in the middle of your sentence. You can create actual error either by inadvertent, treacherous placement of a word or phrase, or by ambiguous modification in the sentence. (Stay with us here: below is a step-by-step explanation of those terms.)

Treacherous placement of a word or phrase can have serious consequences. Unfortunately, it is easy to inadvertently toss onto a page something that pops into your mind without delaying your legal analysis while you think through the very words you need. In the same way, you will create ambiguity if you allow a *word to modify the wrong word* or if you allow the words to wander away from *exactly* where they need to be. Think Funny Headlines: "Man Shot by His House," or, "Two Sisters Reunite after 18 Years in the Check-Out Line." In the context of a legal document, these types of mistakes may provide your readers with moments of great hilarity, and they will wind up embarrassing you.

If that's not enough to worry about, here is an additional warning about sentence errors: if you don't create *parallel constructions* for your parallel ideas, then readers can—and probably will—misunderstand the intent of the sentence.

Below you will find a checklist of editing solutions to cure some of these errors.

SOLUTIONS

1. Place modifiers precisely—**directly before or directly after** the word (antecedent) or word groups (antecedents) they modify.

Consider this sentence:

We offered the auctioneer an antique desk and chair to auction off at the law school charity event.

When the auctioneer goes to auction the goods, will he be auctioning off two antiques, or merely an antique desk with a not-so-antique chair? In our situation, which was a real-life event, the auctioneer believed he was getting two antiques while we believed we had been quite clear in offering one antique that went along with a chair that was not antique. The auctioneer was not happy.

As you see, ambiguity is inherent in the English language. If you are aware that it's out there, you can re-read drafts specifically hunting for modifiers and the nouns that they should be attached to. We had to face only an angry auctioneer; you might be facing an angry client and a confused judge. Every day, courts are forced to interpret contract clauses with modifiers floating among several nouns. Now is the time to learn good editing habits: when you read your own material, you may notice that even *you* are unsure where the modifier goes—that's a bad sign for your legal analysis.

Look at the dilemma created below by a tiny, limiting modifier ("only"):

> He shot himself in the foot Monday.
> *Only* **he** shot himself in the foot Monday.
> He *only* **shot** himself in the foot Monday.
> He shot *only* **himself** in the foot Monday.
> He shot himself *only* **in the foot** Monday.
> He shot himself in the foot *only* **Monday.**
> He shot himself in the foot Monday *only*.

The six sentences have vastly different meanings that have been created merely by the placement of one word. This investigation of word placement is not only the "art" of legal writing, but, depending on the document you are drafting, the necessity. Thus, the moral of the story is that when you are writing legal documents, choose the placement of your modifiers very carefully, even the "little" modifiers.[2]

2. **Evaluate** each modifier that a reader might interpret to **modify more than one** noun.

To correct an ambiguity, you might add a limiting article (a, an, the); break the sentence into two; separate the nouns (antecedents) being modified; or provide other clarifying information.

Consider these examples:

☒ For the law school charity auction, we will give you an antique desk and chair.

☑ For the law school charity auction, we will give you an antique desk and **a** recently purchased lawn chair.

---

[2] For examples of treacherous placement of words that have been litigated in court, see Terri LeClercq, *Doctrine of the Last Antecedent*, 2 J. LEGAL WRITING INST. 81 (1996).

☑ For the law school charity auction, we will give you an antique desk. We are giving you a chair, too.

☑ For the law school charity auction, we will give you an antique desk **from Maine**, and also one of our cherished mahogany lawn chairs.

3. Watch for **dangling elements. Dangling elements** are pieces of the sentences that seem to point to concrete antecedents but, in actuality, modify something that isn't even in the sentence. Grammarians refer to these constructions as "dangling elements" because a reader can't connect the phrase with anything explicitly inside the words of the sentence:

☒ Reading multiple books a day, the library was always a great place to concentrate. (Who is reading? It's not the library reading, is it?)

☑ Because **I** read multiple books a day, the library was always a great place to concentrate.

☑ Reading multiple books a day, **I** always sat in the library, a great place to concentrate.

4. Learn the difference between "**that**" and "**which.**" In any technical field, precision is essential. Legal writing is a branch of technical writing, a branch that requires writers to concentrate on words for both present and future implications. Thus, you need to become a stickler for exact wording. One constant source of confusion is the difference between essential and nonessential information within a sentence. Word choice helps readers evaluate what is essential (as does Punctuation, Chapter 4).

"That" signals that material following immediately is essential to meaning. "Which" signals that the following information is nonessential to the meaning of the sentence. Now: which sentence below indicates that I have more than one version of a will?

a) You should read my will that is in the bottom drawer.

b) You should read my will, which is in the bottom drawer.

In **a)**, I am directing you to a will, *the will in the drawer* (distinguished by the word choice from one, say, in the safe). But in **b)**, I have only one will, one that (by the way) is in the bottom drawer. Although you will frequently see these words used interchangeably, they might create ambiguity. Learn this distinction now.

5. Keep listed items in your sentence **parallel.** This admonition means that, when creating lists, you should structure similar elements within a list the same.

Desiree's daily job with the International Labor Organization included **creating an inventory** of past issues and **assistance** with current European cases. ("creating" is an -ing verb; "assistance" is a noun)

Desiree's daily job with the International Labor Organization included **creating an inventory** of past issues and **assisting with** current European cases. (both are now -ing verbs)

a. Also review your **numbered lists for** grammatically parallel items. Again, the key here is "parallel."

The government required the international oil company 1) to stop the massive underwater leak, 2) to clean up the ocean and the beach of spilled oil, and 3) compensation to businesses for both lost income and the wages of now unemployed workers. (1 and 2 are parallel verb infinitives, but 3 is a noun.)

The government required the international oil company 1) **to stop** the massive underwater leak, 2) **to clean** up the ocean and the beach of spilled oil, and 3) **to compensate** businesses for both lost income and the wages of now unemployed workers.

b. More difficult but equally important is to keep items parallel that follow **correlative conjunctions.** A correlative conjunction is a pair of conjunctions that grammatically link equal elements: either . . . or; neither . . . nor; not only . . . but also; whether . . . or; both . . . and.

When correlative conjunctions are not used with their proper "partner," the reader senses a certain dissonance, like hearing a bad note in a musical chord:

The law review candidate neither researched the article properly or used proper citation format.

The law review candidate **neither researched** the article properly **nor used** the proper citation format.

Correlative conjunctions may also present problems when they are not placed properly in a sentence:

Not only were the first-year law students afraid of the new professors **but also** their third-year classmates. (Were the first-year students afraid of their professors and their third-year classmates, or were the first-year students and their third-year classmates afraid of the new professors?)

The first-year students were afraid **not only** of the new professors **but also** of their third-year classmates.

c. Finally, avoid confusing readers about your parallel elements when you **inadvertently repeat** "that" in a string of clauses.

The plagiarist said **that** because he had worked with these papers over the summer **that** the material was not strictly classified.

The plagiarist said **that** because he had worked with the papers over the summer the material was not strictly classified.

6. Beware of **multiple pronoun antecedents.**

The concept of "multiple pronoun antecedents" is a fancy way of saying that you have created a sentence that has multiple people doing multiple things. Make sure you're clear in describing Who Does What to Whom.

While arguing with her own attorney, she also told the judge that she abused the legal system. (Who has abused the legal system? The "she," and just who is "she"? The judge? Maybe the attorney? We need the pronoun attached to, or replaced by, one of the nouns to give the sentence clarity.)

While arguing with her own attorney, **the defendant** also told the judge that **even the judge** abused the legal system.

Similar to multiple pronoun antecedents, **vague referents** make unclear pronoun references to nouns or groups of actions in the sentence. The vagueness may occur when multiple things are going on in the sentence. Here are some examples and how they might be fixed:

The professors told the students that they would learn a lot this year. (Exactly who will be learning a lot? The students? The professors?)

The professors told the students that the students would be learning a lot this year. (or that the faculty always learns a lot, too)

The professor told us that it was going to be a challenge. (What was going to be a challenge?)

The professor told us that Legal Writing was going to be a challenge.

7. Investigate the antecedents of **demonstrative and relative pronouns.** "Demonstrative" pronouns point back to nouns: this, these, that, those. "Relative" pronouns are similar, but they function to introduce clauses: who, whom, whose, which, that. Here's where these pronouns create trouble in legal writing: after a sentence or paragraph, writers begin the next sentence with "This," or the next phrase with "which" and assume readers understand which noun or idea back in the previous sentence the writer is referring to.

This ambiguity can cause reader confusion and legal entanglements:

The Model Code of Professional Responsibility provides that a lawyer may not "threaten to present criminal charges solely to obtain an advantage in a civil matter." DR 7-105. **This** would focus lawyers for both sides on the actual issue. (What would focus the lawyers on the actual issue?)

The Model Code of Professional Responsibility provides that a lawyer may not "threaten to present criminal charges solely to obtain an advantage in a civil matter." DR 7-105. **This limitation** (*or* **This restriction**) would focus lawyers for both sides on the actual issue.

A lawyer may not "threaten to present criminal charges solely to obtain an advantage in a civil matter," **which** keeps lawyers on both sides focused on the issue. (What is keeping them focused?)

A lawyer may not "threaten to present criminal charges solely to obtain an advantage in a civil matter," a **limitation that** keeps (*or* **a restriction** that keeps) lawyers on both sides focused on the issue.

8. Keep **noun and pronoun substitutes** parallel to reflect parallel ideas and parallel structures. Sometimes an *additional* pronoun in a sentence will confuse the reader as to which items are supposed to be parallel. Likewise, sometimes a *missing* pronoun may cause the same type of confusion.

The **rule** represents poor policy, is open to constitutional challenge, and **it** violates due process. ("It" repeats the introductory noun and makes it unclear whether the writer is still talking about the rule or maybe is making a vague reference to something else that may have appeared in a previous sentence.)

The **rule represents** poor policy, **is open** to constitutional challenge, **and violates** due process.

Thus, the court **held that** the complaint was not vague or conclusory **and it** was "adequate to give notice of the claims asserted."

Thus, the court **held that** the complaint was not vague or conclusory **and that** it was "adequate to give notice of the claims asserted."

Try These

EXERCISE 2. AVOIDING ERROR

The answers to Exercise 2 can be found on page 97.

Examine and correct the placement of modifiers in these sentences.

1. After researching both primary and secondary sources, law review drafts are reviewed by the editorial board.

2. The court only reversed the conviction for murder, but sustained the conviction for breaking and entering.

Rewrite the following sentences, replacing ambiguous pronouns or otherwise making the sentences clear.

3. The client asked him if he had to tell him the complete truth and whether this would affect their relationship.

4. While the client was speaking, the attorney seemed to develop a headache as well as have fears about taking the case, so the client had to find a way to ameliorate it before he could reveal a few more of the facts of his story.

Redo these sentences as necessary to create parallel items within them.

5. When arguing before the court, new attorneys must remember:

a. to dress appropriately;
b. to address the court directly;
c. that all members of the staff are part of the court; and
d. that time is limited.

6. A patient may have a cause of action against a doctor if the doctor examined him, determined he was an appropriate candidate for an experimental treatment, made hospital arrangements, but in the haste of the consultation, not informing the patient of the risk associated with this experimental treatment.

INCORPORATING AUTHORITY

Legal writing is characterized by its need for, and excessive use of, authority. This tension is first a surprise and then a constant challenge to legal writers. *Intruding citations* may create stumbling blocks for readers. A poorly placed or awkwardly introduced citation may distract the reader from the substance of your sentence. However, citations are necessary. Indeed, the expectation of the legal reader is to see citations in certain positions and to see a lot of them. Nonetheless, there are methods for improving the style of your sentences by your introductions to your cases, and by you placement of citations.

A second common problem for those who read legal documents is the incorporation of *lengthy quotations*. Keep in mind what we said earlier in this chapter: judges often write legal opinions in such a way that the reasoning is obscured. If your job as the legal writer is to interpret these obscure opinions, then why would you choose to directly quote difficult language? Nonetheless, struggling first-year students often do just that.

Why?

Well, there are various reasons. First, novice law students are afraid of getting it wrong, so what better way to get it right than to repeat exactly what the judge said? Second, first-year students spend a lot of time hearing about how plagiarism is bad. What better way to avoid plagiarizing than to quote an opinion exactly, rather than to "steal" a few words and try to incorporate them in your own writing? Finally, often professors will advise students to use direct language rather than putting material in their own words.

All of these justifications for directly quoting passages cause problems for the reader who is trying to understand the substance of your paper. In the first place, if you quote directly, you're not creating a document that has a consistent style—your own. Plus, each direct quote is required to begin and end with quotation marks. Line after line of quoted material is obvious to the reader and highlights that material has been cut and pasted. When you have shifting writing styles, a reader is forced to shift perspectives, as if reading a play. As long as you properly cite any paraphrasing, it is fine to paraphrase—except for key words in opinions and statutes.

The purpose of memo writing is to *briefly* explain the law. Lengthy direct quotations rarely help to do that. However, if you decide it is essential to use a lengthy quotation, make sure that there is some context for the quotation. A long quotation that appears without any introductory material disrupts the textual discussion.

Take this sentence, from a case dealing with restrictions on speech:

> In *Sawyer v. Sandstorm*, 615 F.2d 311, 317 (5th Cir. 1980), the court held, "[e]ven though the governmental purpose [may] be legitimate and substantial, that purpose cannot be pursued by means that broadly stifle fundamental personal liberties when the end can be more narrowly achieved."

What did the court hold? It seems as though the court held that the First Amendment right to free speech does not allow the government to restrict speech by enacting broad prohibitions, when what the government is really trying to restrict may be achieved by something much more specific and narrow. If so, why not quote only the essential language and paraphrase the rest?

Here are some solutions to problems regarding incorporating authority and lengthy quotes into your writing:

SOLUTIONS

1. Avoid **awkward citation placement**.

Legal readers expect to see case citations located in certain places and introduced in specific ways. When your discussion is focused on a particular case, the reader expects to see the name of the case and its citation in the sentence. However, there is a correct and an incorrect way to incorporate the case.

Take this sentence:

> *Office of Disciplinary Counsel v. Surrick*, 750 A.2d 441 (Pa. 2007), maintained that the plagiarism charges should apply to the Ph.D. defendant.

What's the problem? The problem is that it is the citation itself that is the "actor" in the sentence. You need to ensure that it is the court that is the main "actor" in the sentence. You have several options to avoid the stylistic problem.

a. When introducing cases in a sentence, **move** the citation to a prepositional phrase:

In *Office of Disciplinary Counsel v. Surrick*, 750 A.2d 441 (Pa. 2007), the court maintained that the plagiarism charges should apply to the Ph.D. defendant.

In some instances, the case itself is not the focal point of the sentence; rather, the general idea within the case is the focal point. If the case's idea is the intended purpose of the sentence, then you can use another stylistic tool to improve your writing. Thus:

b. **Move** citations to the end of your sentences where appropriate.

The general rule in Pennsylvania is that an allegation of plagiarism may also result in a federal criminal charge. *Office of Disciplinary Counsel v. Surrick*, 750 A.2d 441 (Pa. 2007).

c. **Avoid** ending one sentence with a citation and beginning the next sentence with another citation; construct sentences so that there is some separation between full citations.

Texas courts allow the university general counsel to determine the validity of student plagiarism charges. *Student Ethics Committee v. Piddleheimer*, 150 S.W.3d 888 (Tex. 2007). *Office of Disciplinary Counsel v. Surrick*, 750 A.2d 441 (Pa. 2007), is a Pennsylvania case dealing with a similar situation.

Texas courts allow the university general counsel to determine the validity of student plagiarism charges. *Student Ethics Committee v. Piddleheimer*, 150 S.W.3d 888 (Tex. 2007). **A Pennsylvania court** discussed a similar concept in *Office of Disciplinary Counsel v. Surrick*, 750 A.2d 441 (Pa. 2007).

d. **Separate** citations that appear as authority for one sentence and use the case name as the main subject of the next sentence.

Texas courts allow university general counsel to determine the validity of student plagiarism charges. *Student Ethics Committee v. Piddleheimer*, 150 S.W.3d 888 (Tex. 2007). In that case, the court dealt with the allegation that several graduate students had plagiarized their Ph.D. theses. *Id.* at 892.

Texas courts allow university general counsel to determine the validity of student plagiarism charges. *Student Ethics Committee v. Piddleheimer*, 150 S.W.3d 888 (Tex. 2007). **In the case of *Piddleheimer*,** the court dealt with the allegation that several graduate students had plagiarized their Ph.D. theses. *Id.* at 892.

One more thing: some judges and law professors favor putting all citations in footnotes. In the opinion of many, this method of citation is less distracting for the reader. However, be forewarned that this method is not commonplace in practice. Thus, the question of citation placement is one of those questions that is best answered by making sure that you are following the instructions of your boss—whether that boss is the one who pays your salary, or the one who has assigned a particular writing assignment.

2. Avoid **excessive/intrusive quotations**.

When using a direct quotation, question the purpose of including each long quotation. Paraphrase lengthy quotes.

Ask:

Do I need the full quotation?
Does it convey what I want to convey?
Does the reader have to interpret the quote, or have I interpreted the meaning for the reader?

Use quotations that "flow" within your normal pattern of communicating information. That is, would you utter that quote yourself if you were explaining the law to someone else? Legal concepts in the direct quote, but they should work it around the information that they choose to convey:

In *Sawyer v. Sandstorm*, 615 F.2d 311, 317 (5th Cir. 1980), the court held that even when the government has a "legitimate and substantial" purpose in restricting speech, it may not do so if what is intended to be restricted can be "more narrowly achieved" by other means.

Try These

EXERCISE 3. INCORPORATING AUTHORITY

The answers to Exercise 3 can be found on page 98.

Identify the style problem in each sentence. Then move or correct the following citations using the above suggestions.

1. *United States v. Frost*, 125 F.3d 346 (6th Cir. 1997), originally set forth the test for proving the cause of action against the defendants.

2. The Supreme Court made its decision regarding suppressing favorable evidence in *Brady v. Maryland*, 373 U.S. 83 (1963). *Kyles v. Whitley*, 514 U.S. 419 (1995), reviewed the materiality requirement and held that a "touchstone of materiality is a reasonable probability of a different result."

Translate or paraphrase the quotes in the following examples to ensure that the intended meaning of the sentence is clear:

3. In dicta, the court stated, "the existence of the waiver [of one's right to privacy] carries with it the right to an invasion of privacy only to such an extent as may be legitimately necessary and proper in dealing with the matter which has brought about the waiver." *Pavesich v. New England Life Ins. Co.*, 50 S.E. 68, 72 (Ga. 1905).

4. The court acknowledged that "a legal search of an individual's person is contingent on numerous factors including the reason and experience of the law enforcement officer who has made a stop of the person." *Terry v. Ohio*, 392 U.S. 1, 27 (1968).

What to Remember

- Review **sentence length,** keeping sentences as short as their meanings will allow.
- Place your **verbs close** to their subjects.
- Keep any initial **dependent clause short,** or move it behind the main clause.
- Review sentences to keep **modifiers close** to the noun they modify.
- Review sentences and eliminate **unnecessary detail.**
- Use **dovetailing** for clarity and grace.
- Avoid **vague references** to nouns previously introduced in a sentence.
- Create **parallel** structure to highlight parallel ideas.
- Review each sentence and **revise unnecessary passive** voice.
- Keep only **necessary quotations** and paraphrase the others.
- Make sure that quotes are introduced with a **context.**

♦ ♦ ♦ ♦

Cleansed of words without meaning, much of the language of the law need not be peculiar at all. And better for it.

David Mellinkoff, The Language of the Law 454 (1963).

♦ ♦ ♦ ♦

3 CHOOSING WORDS WITH STYLE

Every writer dreams of creating elegant, flowing sentences. Undoubtedly some writers can achieve elegance with little effort. Usually, though, in the first years of law school, writers struggle to grasp legal concepts, to draft them onto a page, to create coherence with law and facts, and to write intelligibly.

This chapter will help you sharpen your word choice and eliminate flab. What emerges may, indeed, be elegance. It will certainly be more professional. You may not be aware of it, but word choice in both conversation and writing reflects your personal style.

Look at your draft again (you may notice that we say that a lot), and examine each sentence to ensure that it says exactly what you intended. It will come as no surprise that precise word choice can mean the difference between success and failure. So, repeat the mantra: Who Did What to Whom? Keeping that in mind, you will edit flabby words and replace them with deliberate, strong nouns and strong verbs.

As you repeat the Who Did What to Whom, you can return to the question of intended audience. Just as you consciously chose sentence structures that targeted your message to the intended audience, now you need to hone your word choice. Will a layman client read this letter? Will your supervising attorney review this memo? Will court personnel and your client read this filing?

Audience matters.

Let's see how to choose words for professional audiences by focusing on jargon and terms of art, strong nouns and verbs, nominalizations, wordiness, and treacherous/misused words.

JARGON AND TERMS OF ART

Every profession has its share of **jargon**, that specialized vocabulary used within a group that has common backgrounds or interests. Naturally, the use of jargon can save time when it is understood by everyone within that group. Unfortunately, it can baffle those outside that intended group; you could be wasting outsiders' time and also creating confusion—and ultimately irritation.

Terms of art, on the other hand, are an insider's shorthand to underlying concepts. Attorneys depend on terms of art for daily communication among themselves: *dictum*, *garnishment*, *fee simple*. Law students learn these terms as a shorthand for the legal concepts they are studying. But readers untrained in the law cannot be expected to understand these terms. Interestingly, many specialized words within one area of law confuse even other lawyers.

Seasoned legal writers may inadvertently use these specialized words and phrases in documents for laymen because they forget that others aren't familiar with the terms and their underlying concepts. Both your use of jargon and your use of legal terms of art will be contingent on **audience**. Your ultimate goal is to craft an understandable discussion for your anticipated audience: your professor on an exam; the judge or your classmates; or your client who has a legal background, as distinguished from your client who does not have a legal background.

Remember, many concepts in the law are longstanding and were developed through old cases at a time when only the clergy and learned legal advisors comprised the audience; legal language was expected to reflect formal language. Now, however, both the law and language have changed, and your audience expects wording to be clear and to the point. Thus, improve your word choice by weeding out any inadvertent **archaic legalisms** (words with contemporary, plain English equivalents) for *all* your audiences.

For instance, "herein" usually means "in this document" and can be written that way. If you realize that it doesn't mean "in this document" in your draft, you have an even stronger reason to change the wording other than replacing "legalese." And when you realize that you've repeated words from your casebooks like *viz*, scratch them immediately. Let's be honest;

you don't know what *viz* means, and its ambiguity can lead you into trouble. Court cases prove that even experienced attorneys and judges can't tell if its modern equivalent, "namely," is inclusive or exclusive. Leave Latin for those who read Latin.

While weeding your draft for word choice, also search for **coupled synonyms**, which were customary hundreds of years ago when three languages (French, Latin, and versions of Old English) were used simultaneously. We all don't speak Latin and French today, so try to find a suitable alternative to a coupled synonym. However, keep in mind: some of them are necessary, so do your homework before you delete. You can probably reduce "each and every" to "each" without changing your meaning, but look at "bequeath and devise." In legal history, people "bequeathed" personal property; they "devised" real property. Whew! Suddenly you can see that word choice involves more than a review of grammar and punctuation rules. Word choice reflects both your audience and the legal concepts you learn each day.

Here's a list of coupled synonyms that you might consider simplifying. Keep in mind, however, that some coupled words may be customarily used in specialized fields of law (for example, "Last Will and Testament"). Your audience may prefer a coupled synonym even if you believe that the terms are redundant and unnecessary.

aid and abet	act and deed
authorize and empower	annul and set aside
deem and consider	absolutely and completely
covenant and agree	free and unfettered
each and every	each and all
excess and unnecessary	false and untrue
final and conclusive	full and complete
fit and proper	have and hold
for and in consideration of	force and effect
in truth and in fact	void and of no effect
for and enduring	save and except
for and in consideration of	give, devise, and bequeath
keep and maintain	last will and testament
truth and veracity	lot, tract, or parcel of land
modified or changed	null, void, and of no effect
order and direct	ordered, judged, and decreed

PROFESSIONAL TONE

Jargon and terms of art are word-choice decisions that can be made when you construct a legal document. Professional tone relates to word choice, but a different type of word choice—a choice that helps ensure that you appropriately represent yourself in a professional field.

The world has become less formal. Men no longer wear fedoras to baseball games, as we sometimes see in newsreels and movies from the 1940s. Women rarely show up at the family breakfast table wearing a dress and with make-up, as we see in the 1960s' television shows. Few people now dress up to take a plane, and the description "business casual" is a well-known phrase in our vocabulary. Despite the informalities that now exist in our society, many formal conventions still exist, especially in relation to writing in a professional manner. Those who are in professional careers (like the law, of course) expect the information they receive to meet the expected conventions necessary to address a more serious audience. These conventions include tone and manner in how one communicates with professors, attorneys, courts, and clients.

With the advent of email and text messaging, much of the formality that existed with writing letters has become passé. Rules regarding spelling, capitalization, and punctuation are relaxed when you communicate by email, and especially when you communicate by text messaging.

But remember, when you enter a professional environment, you must revert to a more formal method of communication. You should not use any computer short-cuts when engaged in an exchange (even an email exchange) with a professional colleague. The letter "r" should never be used as a shorthand for "are," and the letter "u" should never be used as a shorthand for "you." Even current, widely accepted abbreviations (e.g., "btw" for "by the way," or "thnx" for "thanks," or "IMHO" for "in my humble opinion") should be used only in informal exchanges and only in situations where you are sure that the recipient 1) understands the abbreviations, 2) is comfortable with their use, and 3) expects informality from you in the role of communicator (rather than, say, an attorney). Remember that many of the people who are now in positions of power did not grow up with text messaging or even using email. Make sure that you are accommodating their expectations with appropriate, formal written communication. This admonition includes not only email messages answering inquiries from a boss, but also email communications with your law professors.

In addition to the editing strategies above, you can make a more understandable and more interesting document if you focus on the categories below:

- Weak nouns and flabby verbs
- Nominalizations
- Circumlocution and Elegant Variation
- Wordiness
- Treacherous words

WEAK NOUNS AND FLABBY VERBS

Attorneys may nod off after reading documents a few hours—who can blame them? Lots of pages, lots of citations, and few, very few Who Did What to Whom sentences. You can make your writing both more credible and more precise if you edit for concrete nouns and action verbs. How many readers nod off while following a story in *Sports Illustrated*? Action verbs! Concrete nouns! Of course insurance law or an estate question doesn't have a lineman breaking through to the quarterback, but if you'll check *Sports Illustrated*, you'll find a number of enticing articles about players who have lost The Big One (plaintiff loses estate?) and how to retain fan loyalty (estate planning?). The point is this: when you are fine-tuning your legal document, you should take time and take care with words.

SOLUTIONS

1. **Eliminate vague and ambiguous** references by substituting concrete references where necessary.

Although the party complained about the court's decision, it was decided that the facts were uncontested. (Which party? What decision? Who decided the facts were uncontested?)

Although the defendant, Mr. Gutierrez[3], complained about the court's granting Summary Judgment, the record proved that the facts were uncontested.

In this case, one must prove intent.

The **State must prove** intent.

[3] A party's name should not be used until it is accompanied by a description of who the party is in a case, e.g., the defendant, the plaintiff, etc. . . . However, at least one court requires that the party names—rather than party designation—be used in documents filed with the courts. Wis. Stat. Rule. 809.19(a) (i).

2. Replace **unnecessary deadwood** (expletives), e.g., “there is,” “there are,” and “it is.” They can weaken the force of the sentence.

There is no reason a famous lawyer should have to spend time on this nonsense.

A famous lawyer would not waste time on this nonsense.

Caveat: Of course, some sentences need to begin with “there is”: “There is no reason to worry about the indictment today.” It would be clumsy and even wordier to apply a hard-and-fast editing rule and thus create a monster: “No reason exists to worry about that indictment today.”

3. Avoid **circumlocution** and **elegant variation.** With circumlocution, writers waste an enormous number of words to say something that could be said more simply. With elegant variation, writers try to display their wide vocabulary, changing “auto” to “car” to “vehicle” and thus muddy the waters. Remember that in law school you get extra credit neither for the number of words you use nor for the difficulty and variety of those words. The goal is clarity. You are not trying to hide meaning under a barrage of verbiage that only law-school graduates can decipher.

The person who is positioned in the front left of the vehicle should always wear his seatbelt.

The driver should always wear his seatbelt.

She was expecting a government individual who had specialty in reviewing tax returns.

She was expecting an IRS agent.

NOMINALIZATIONS

Many a strong verb or concrete noun is hidden beneath **nominalizations**, those multisyllabic words with Latinate suffixes and prefixes:

-ize	-osity
-ate	-ability
-tion	-ancy
-ion	-al
-ence	-ive
-ment	mis-

Some examples are investiga**tion**, necess**itate**, intellig**ence**, **mis**appropriate. Although grammatically correct, nominalizations may dilute a sentence by implying, rather than stating, the logical who/what relationships in the sentence.

One of the ACLU lawyers made an **investigation** of the original filing.

An ACLU lawyer **investigated** the original filing.

Despite the attorney's **mischaracterization** of the law, the jury still reached the **conclusion** that the defendant was guilty.

Although the attorney **characterized** the law incorrectly, the jury still **concluded** that the defendant was guilty.

SOLUTIONS

1. Watch for and replace nouns created **from stronger verbs:**

Nominalization	**Verb Form**
determination	to determine
resolution	to resolve
utilization	to use
reinforcement	to reinforce
the addition of	to add
assumption	to assume
continuation	to continue

2. Also watch for and replace some nouns created from **adjectives** (that are themselves once stronger verbs):

Noun/Adjective	**Original Verb**
enforceability/enforceable	enforce
applicability/applicable	apply
specificity/specific	specify

WORDINESS

Including the requisite statement of facts and relevant case law already guarantees length. You don't have to worry about dogmatically filling 10 pages any more, as you did in undergraduate school. So you must un-learn the successful technique of tossing in as many words as possible just to fill space. Look at your casebooks—and remember that these are summaries or cut-down versions of the original opinions. Yes. And think back to other legal documents you've read. Those legal documents frequently read as if the office copier has accidentally duplicated previous paragraphs.

Verbal flab results in lengthy documents and uninteresting readings, so focus on your drafts with a hungry eye. Think about "who" (strong noun) "did what" (strong verb) to "whom" (strong noun). Then imagine how much more forceful your prose will be if you **cut a fourth of your remaining material** from your draft with the following techniques.

SOLUTIONS

1. Omit unnecessary **prepositions.**

Fred Fender read **through** the ACLU complaint **with regard to** the employee-salary procedures **of** his clients. (16 words)

Fred Fender read the ACLU's complaint **about** his clients' employee-salary procedures. (11 words)

A provision of the employee contracts required commission-only compensation. (10 words)

The **employee contracts' provision** required commission-only compensation. (8 words)

2. Omit **throat clearers.** Experienced law professors will tell you that "clearly" and "it is clear" are signals that what follows isn't clear at all. One of your own verbal ticks may be in the list below:

obviously
it would appear to be the case that
as a matter of fact
the fact of the matter is
it is obvious that
if one takes into consideration

Keep in mind, however, that some "throat clearers" serve a stylistic purpose when you are trying to convey a certain tone in a court filing (e.g., "As a matter of fact, the police officer did not even ask the defendant whether he wanted an attorney.") Still, some phrases are merely space-fillers; change them to more direct language.

It would appear to be the case that he hadn't done his own research, but **to tell the truth**, he didn't have the time now to waste responding to the ACLU's complaint. (28 words)

He hadn't done his own research, and he didn't have the time now to waste responding to the ACLU's complaint. (20 words)

The defendant found himself **in a situation where** he became desperate for cash. (13 words)

The defendant was desperate for cash. (6 words)

3. Avoid **unnecessary modification** unless it serves a tactical purpose.

Creatively, he added **a very unique** introduction to **each and every** case the ACLU had cited. (16 words)

Creatively, he added a unique introduction to each case the ACLU had cited. (13 words; perhaps delete "creatively" as redundant)

4. Watch for **redundancy.** If you add a repetitive synonym to strong nouns, you might actually weaken them rather than strengthen them.

Redundant	**Possible Revision**
alleged suspect	suspect
consensus of opinion	consensus
free gift	gift
rather (or most) unique	unique
the said party	that party, the defendants

whether or not[4]	whether
next subsequent	subsequent
personal (or honest) opinion	opinion
single most	most
reason is because	reason is (*or* because)
true facts	facts
such statute	statute, or the statute

TREACHEROUS WORDS

Choosing the exact and necessary word in any type of communication is hard, deliberate work. As was demonstrated in the previous chapter, an incorrect or incorrectly placed word can cause great hilarity to the reader. Some merely cause confusion.

On a recent trip, a friend noticed a sign posted at a drugstore. It read, "We Accept all Competitive Coupons."

Competitive coupons? What does that mean? A competitive coupon could be one that has nice bright colors, or one that specifies a certain amount off. But who decides just what is a competitive coupon? Probably the person who put up the sign meant, "We accept all competitors' coupons."

Some words elude us as we draft; others sound correct in a context but aren't; some words are incorrect in any context. No one knows the meaning of every word or when to use each word he or she does know. But in legal writing, it is essential to review the shades of difference between synonyms, for instance, and to keep track of those words you frequently misuse.

Here are some commonly misused words:

1. **affect/effect:** *Affect* is a verb, meaning to influence or to assume the appearance of. *Effect* is a noun, meaning the result. (*Effect* can also be a

[4] "Whether or not" is usually redundant: *We do not know whether or not the executive summary will bring you immediate benefits (*unnecessary "or not"*).* But like most "rules," this one does not cover all possibilities: *Agency fees are collected to defray expenses of the activities of the union, expenses that benefit all members of the collective bargaining unit, whether union members or not.* Here, the "or not" is syntactically necessary to complete the thought.

verb meaning "to make a change" or "to accomplish.")

A professor's reputation for giving low grades *affects* everyone in her room.

We can see the *effect* of her reputation when students slip into the last rows.

2. **alternative/option, choice:** If you have *two* choices, each is an alternative to the other. Traditionally, linguists have held that with more than two options, you have *options* or *choices* but not an *alternative.* (Many contemporary linguists no longer hold tightly to this distinction, but some still do.)

3. **among/between:** *Among* refers to groups of three or more; *between* functions as a distinction between only two.

Among the many functions of a lawyer is taking yearly CLE courses. *Between* client pressure and billing-hours pressure, some lawyers are tempted to cut ethical corners.

Between and *among* require objective pronouns:

Between you and *me*, I can't stand to witness fights between *him* and *her*. So among *us*, the custom is to bring cookies to the office once a week.

4. **Because/as:** *As* is a comparative, like *like. Because* signals causality.

Because he didn't attend many classes, his classmates thought he had dropped the course.

The Defendant can be *as* sincere *as* a nun, but *because* she has her dates wrong, she will not be believed.

5. **assume/presume:** To *assume* is to take for granted that something is true or accurate. To *presume* is to take upon oneself without leave or warrant, to dare or go beyond what is right or proper. Note the use of the root in *presumption.*

6. **assure/insure/ensure:** All three of these words mean to make certain or safe, so their precise use is complicated. You *assure* people (removing doubt or suspense). You *insure* with money and guarantees (and insurance policies). And you *ensure* when you are making things certain or safe (e.g., *ensure* your child's safety with a seat belt).

7. **based on/based off:** Technically, there is no real difference in meaning between *based on* and *based off*, although grammatically, *based off* would need to be followed by an *of*. ("Based off of the recent weather

trends, I can no longer predict what I can wear from day-to-day.") Although use of *based off* has become more popular in recent years, the traditions of legal writing still favor the use of *based on*."

8. **because/since:** *Because* signals a causal relationship; *since* is an indication of time past. Traditionally, these words signaled different meanings and were not interchangeable, but now that general distinction has changed. However, be aware that your reader may find the technical difference between the two important.

9. **bimonthly/semimonthly:** Most writers resort to using "every two months" or "twice a month." Nevertheless, *bi* means two; *semi* means half. Thus, *bimonthly* is every two months, and *semimonthly* is twice a month.

10. **composed/comprised:** *Composed* means made of (the parts compose the whole), and *comprised* means contains (the whole comprises the parts).

    The audience is *composed of* people with varied backgrounds.
    The symphony hall *comprises* people with varied backgrounds.

11. **connotation/denotation:** A *connotation* is an implication, while a *denotation* points out something specific. Ordinarily, *denotation* is not used as a noun but is more commonly used as a verb.

    The *connotation* of the pleadings is that the plaintiff was discharged on the basis of age discrimination.
    The relevant provisions of the contract are *denoted* by yellow highlighting.

12. **continuous/continual:** *Continual* means frequently occurring; *continuous* means occurring without interruption.

    The lawyer had to sit through a two-hour, *continuous* CLE on ethics.
    A disgruntled participant in the back row offered *continual* interruptions.

13. **contest/attest:** To *contest* means to object to something, while *attest* means to declare that something exists or is accurate.

    She *attested* to the fact that she is a citizen of the United States.
    He did not *contest* that fact.

14. currently/presently: Although the nouns *current* and *present* are basically synonymous, the adverb forms traditionally signal a difference in time.

We are *currently* (right now) studying word choice.
Presently (in the very near future) we will stop and take a break.

15. different than/different from: Things *differ from* each other. *Different than* is considered incorrect unless using "from" creates bulky, illogical phraseology following it.

Fender's brief was not *different from* the ACLU's.
I agree that the Supreme Court has interpreted the United States Constitution very *differently than* the Founders intended and that courts err on the side of tyranny.

A rewrite to replace "differently than" would be wordier:

I agree that the Supreme Court has interpreted the United States Constitution differently from the way that the Founders intended and that courts err on the side of tyranny.

16. discreet/discrete: A *discreet* investigator is tactful and judicious, careful. In contrast, an investigator may be *discrete* from other witnesses at the trial, meaning that he is disconnected from them, separate and distinct.

17. disinterested/uninterested: To be *disinterested* is to have no personal involvement. To be *uninterested* is to have a lack of interest.

Kalim was *disinterested* in the outcome of the Super Bowl because her favorite team had been eliminated in the playoffs.
The law student was totally *uninterested* in the guest lecturer, so she fell asleep.

18. duplicitous/duplicative: *Duplicitous* means, essentially, that a person is "two-faced," while *duplicative* means that there are copies of the same thing.

The woman lied to her third husband and was *duplicitous* about her private savings.
The attorney who filed in two different courts simultaneously filed *duplicative* pleadings.

19. hopefully: Traditionally, *hopefully* functioned as an adverb meaning "with hope." Thus, "Hopefully it will rain" implied that the speaker is hoping for rain or, technically, that "it will rain hope." Today, speakers and dictionaries track the word to also mean "I or we hope." Because the option produces an ambiguity, careful writers might want to stick to the traditional rule to limit its use.

20. however: *However* is a conjunctive adverb that distinguishes previous material or ideas from the next ones. It is placed where writers need to create a disjunction or emphasis.

He told me the secret; *however*, I had heard the gist of it before.
He told me the secret; I had, *however*, heard it before.
He told me the secret; I had heard it before, *however*.

However should not be used as a mere transition linking two sentences that are continuous in a narrative, or demonstrate the result of an action:

 The judge walked into the court room. *However*, he sat down.

 Maricia's inability to drive less than 70 m.p.h. on her Harley earned her another speeding ticket. *However*, she lost her license. (The proper transition could be either, "As a result," or "Consequently.")

21. i.e./e.g.: *I.e. (id est)* means "that is" and indicates that an inclusive list or statement will follow. *E.g. (exempli gratia)* means "for example" and signals that the author is including an example or examples with the introductory statement. Each is followed by a comma.

Lawyers must accept responsibility for the success of the firm; i.e., they must find clients, perform some research and writing, and keep track of billable hours. (These three distinct acts will represent all of the responsibility.)

Lawyers must accept some responsibility for the success of the firm; e.g., they must find clients. (One of perhaps many aspects of a lawyer's responsibilities.)

22. imply/infer: To *imply* is to hint at something. To *infer* is to suggest an intimate or incriminating connection.

He *implied* that she was not telling the truth when he asked to see her list of references.

He *inferred* there was a high level of hostility in the room.

23. it's/its: *It's* easy to distinguish these two forms if you can remember that the apostrophe signals that a letter is left out, so the form *it's* has to be an abbreviation for *it is*. Following that rule will force its competitor, *its*, into its only logical slot, as a third-person singular pronoun without an apostrophe like other pronouns such as *his* or *her*.

24. lay/lie: *Lay* means to place or put and usually takes an object (transitive verb). Past tense: laid. Perfect: laid. *Lie* means recline (intransitive verb). Past tense: lay. Perfect: lain.

She *laid* her casebooks on the table.
He *lay* awake all night before the exam.

25. negligible/negligent: *Negligible* means a small amount, while *negligent* is a careless act.

The Company claimed that the impact on the environment was *negligible*.

British Petroleum was accused of being *negligent* when it hired numerous subcontractors for the deep-water drilling.

26. prescribe/proscribe: You *prescribe* when you are giving a remedy or a decree. The opposite is true of *proscribe*, when you are forbidding, prohibiting.

27. reluctant/reticent: If a law student is *reluctant* to join a study group, he is unwilling or will grudgingly consent. That he is *reticent*, however, means he does not reveal his feelings readily.

28. seminal/Seminole: *Seminal* means contributing to later development (e.g., the *seminal* case). *Seminole* is a Native American tribe that has its roots in what is now Florida. It is rare (but, of course, possible) that a first year student will be writing about a *Seminole* case.

29. subsequently/consequently: *Subsequently* means following in time, while *consequently* means the result of an action.

Various protesters were arrested at the city center. Many, but not all, were *subsequently* released.

Jonquille passed up the driveway to the courthouse. *Consequently*, she had to make a u-turn at next intersection in the road.

30. that/which: When you draft an essential (restrictive) clause that will not be "punctuated out" of the sentence with commas, use *that*. When you want the information to be merely descriptive, nonessential to the sentence's meaning, use two commas and *which*.

The clause *that* explained the rule is not punctuated.

The clause, *which* merely offered the background of the rule, disappeared from the main text because it was set off with commas.

31. who/which: If your antecedent is inanimate (nonhuman), use *that* or *which* as a pronoun. If the antecedent is a person, use *who*. The question becomes more complicated when you are referring, for instance, to an agency filled with people.

Borrowers were furious with the bank, *which* changed its eligibility formula in the middle of mortgage deals.

Borrowers were furious with the bankers, *who* changed their eligibility formula in the middle of mortgage deals.

SOLUTIONS

1. For other lists of commonly misused words, consult **professional sources** like Wilson Follett, *Modern American Usage: A Guide* (1998); W.H. Fowler, *A Dictionary of Modern English Usage* (2009); and David Mellinkoff, *Mellinkoff's Dictionary of American Legal Usage* (2009).
2. Create **your own list** of words that confuse you or that you frequently misuse. Keep the list in your computer thesaurus or print out a list and keep it near your writing area.
3. When in doubt, **review** the words in this chapter frequently to ensure you understand the differences between easily confused words.
4. **Read** as much as possible whether it be judicial opinions or books. Great readers make great writers.

What to Remember

- Remember your **audience:** Edit for **legal jargon** that is not appropriate, but retain terms of art.
- Avoid **vague references;** use **strong, specific nouns** where possible.
- Delete redundant and **unnecessary words.**
- Avoid **circumlocution** and **elegant variation.**
- Edit to replace **nominalizations.**
- Review our list of frequently **misused words.**
- **Track words** you inadvertently confuse.

Concluding Exercise

The answers to the Concluding Exercise can be found on page 98.

Which of these phrases and sentences can be shortened and yet not substantially changed?

1. He hired an outside company for the purposes of investigating finances.

2. The judge went on to say that he had never seen such a blatant unauthorized use of another's work.

Find common terminology and shorter phrases to replace the following jargon.

3. Fred Fender absolutely refuted the allegations within the indictment. The aforesaid party contended also that he had been unfairly persecuted and enjoined into a morass that his secretary was responsible for.

Identify any nominalizations and rewrite to clarify the who/did what/to whom action that has been implied.

4. A thorough investigation of the two, similar filings necessitated that the clerk work late.

5. The next morning a presentation was made by the clerk to the judge that was full reinforcement of the ACLU's research.

Correct the examples in this concluding quiz that mixes the word problems you've just reviewed. Identify and correct jargon, wordiness, pronoun antecedents, noun strings, nominalizations, and treacherous words.

6. This type and kind of dishonesty reflected on the truth and veracity of any such lawyer and on said court.

7. After researching for any other similar cases, there appear to be several instances of plagiarism in other jurisdictions that the judge discovered and that had been dealt with publicly.

8. The judge found for the ACLU and ordered a strict scrutiny of all of Fender's firm's documents. This was followed by a public announcement.

Circle the correct word.

9. The managing partner, however, had to assure/insure/ensure that the firm was safe from any criticism from the legal community.

10. The firm had continuous/continual CLE classes on ethics.

♦♦♦♦

A world that has only periods is a world without inflections. It is world without shade. It has a music without sharps and flats. It is a martial music. It has a jackboot rhythm. Words cannot bend and curve. A comma, by comparison, changes the gentle drift of the mind in thought, turning in on itself and back on itself, reversing, redoubling and returning along the course of its own sweet river music; while the semicolon brings clauses and thoughts together with all the silent discretion of a hostess arranging guests around her dinner table.

Pico Iyer, *That Humble Comma*, TIME, June 13, 1988, at 80.

♦♦♦♦

4

PUNCTUATING WITH STYLE

Let's return to your draft and this time review the punctuation. Punctuation marks hold together, separate, and set both the pace and the meaning of your document. When early writers added punctuation to their speeches in the third century B.C., they did so to signal places for them to pause when they read aloud. The different marks they developed signaled the reader/speaker's pause length.

Punctuation reflects style when you deliberately choose punctuation marks to reflect your intent. Your intention might be to pushwordstogether or to string them far apart. You may wish to have the reader focus on a word or thought, or you may wish for the reader to skim along. But of course you can't put up deliberate and intrusive signposts in your writing (e.g., "This next sentence is very important."). That's where style comes in—your deliberate choice of marks will make readers speed up, slow down, or pause at appropriate places.

There are not that many punctuation marks and not that many rules for using punctuation marks, but those rules are very important. In attempting to master the art of stylishly punctuating, you must first review and memorize the actual rules below. These rules have been broken into two sets:

- General punctuation rules
- Specific legal-writing punctuation rules

After taking a look at these rules, you can experiment with punctuation options, creating and developing your own style so that readers can learn to depend on your punctuation.

GENERAL PUNCTUATION RULES

1. As you know, **each complete sentence (independent subject and verb) concludes with a period.**

   The basic purpose of the Fourth Amendment is to safeguard the privacy and security of individuals against arbitrary invasion by government officials**.**

2. **Grammatically complete sentences can also be joined/ separated by a semicolon.**

   The basic purpose of the Fourth Amendment is to safeguard the privacy and security of individuals against arbitrary invasion by government officials**;** a search conducted without a warrant based on probable cause is "per se unreasonable" and subject only to "specific and well-defined exceptions." *Katz v. United States*, 389 U.S. 347, 357 (1967).

3. **Complete sentences can also be joined/separated with both a semicolon and a conjunctive adverb.** (therefore, however, nevertheless, consequently, furthermore)

   The basic purpose of the Fourth Amendment is to safeguard the privacy and security of individuals against arbitrary invasion by government officials**; indeed,** a search conducted without a warrant based on probable cause is "per se unreasonable" and subject only to "specific and well-defined exceptions." *Katz v. United States*, 389 U.S. 347, 357 (1967).

4. **An interruptor must be separated "out" of a sentence with commas both before and after it.** (on the other hand, for example, in fact)

If an official**, in fact,** conducts a search pursuant to voluntary consent, then that consent is a legal exception.

5. **Sentences that begin with an adverb (and thus they begin with a dependent clause) require a comma after that clause and before the main subject/verb.** (Although, After, Because, While, When)

When an official conducts a search without a probable-cause warrant**,** that search is "per se unreasonable."

*Note that an adverb cannot stand on its own as a dependent clause:

Although, there are some searches that are "per se unreasonable."

Although many searches are allowed**,** there are some searches that are "per se unreasonable."

6. **Sentences that begin with a short, introductory phrase may—but are not required to—have a comma after the phrase.**

With few exceptions courts may deem the search "reasonable."

With few exceptions**,** courts may deem the search "reasonable."

If, on rereading, you discover that readers might become confused by the lack of a comma, insert one:

Inside a concrete ramp led steeply into a cavern. (readers have to re-read to understand)

Inside**,** a concrete ramp led steeply down into the cavern.

7. **When an adverb clause follows the verb, do not separate the verb from its clause with a comma.** (although, after, because, while, when)

 A search is "per se unreasonable," **when** a search is conducted without a probable-cause warrant.

 A search is "per se unreasonable" **when** a search is conducted without a probable-cause warrant.

8. **Nonessential phrases are set off by commas on either side; essential phrases are not.**

 His companionable dog, Lillie, frequently walked out with his guests. (suggests that Lillie is his only dog or that her name is not essential)

 His companionable dog Lillie frequently walked out with his guests. (no comma around the dog's name; suggests he has more than one dog, and Lillie is the companionable one)

9. **Dates containing both day and year require two commas.**

 The car's driver will appear in court July 15, 2016, to argue the passenger's consent to search the car.

 The car's driver will appear in court July 2016 to argue the passenger's consent to search the car. (contains only a month and year)

10. **Hyphens should be used to combine two adjectives before a noun, or a string of nouns before the main noun.**

 A guilt-ridden passenger had revealed that a knife was hidden under the car seat.

 A ten-cent postage-stamp hike infuriates everyone.Remember, however, that adverbs ending in -ly should never be hyphenated.

 The casually dressed man opened the door to the apartment and backed out immediately.

11. **Dashes should be used to signal a break in thought and writing. (Note that the extended dash, used without a space before or after the mark, is called an "em dash.")**

The driver had refused to consent to the search—even though she had forgotten the knife under her seat.

*Note, dashes may be used instead of commas when the writer wants to add more emphasis to a clause.

Compare:

The officer noticed the red van, an unusual vehicle for this time of night, at the end of the street.

The officer noticed the red van—an unusual vehicle for this time of night—at the end of the street.

Dashes differ from hyphens in both typography and purpose. Dashes are typed with two hyphens and no spaces on either side. Dashes *separate*; hyphens *draw together*.

The driver-side seat was pushed far back. The policeman moved the seat forward—to check beneath it.

12. **Use apostrophes to signal possessives,** not plurals.

The police officers' consent was aimed at both women. (consent of more than one officer)

The driver's refusal came when the officers said they would impound the car. (refusal of only one driver)

English pronouns have their own possessive case (his, my, their, our) and **do not** require an apostrophe.

The United States Supreme Court gave **it's** limitations for the Miranda warnings.

Nouns, including numbers and letters, do not use apostrophes to create plurals.

The occupant's had been speeding in a residential area.

All winners of the 100s were given a one-hundred dollar bill.

I'm just adjusting to the fact that there are two 9:30s in every day.

13. Colons should follow a complete sentence that concludes with a dramatic saying, a list that follows a complete sentence, or a list that completes the sentence.

a. Dramatic saying

Nobel-laureate physicist Lev Landau frequently commented on cosmologists: "They are often in error, but never in doubt."

b. A list that follows a complete sentence

There are five Great Lakes:

1. Lake Erie.
2. Lake Superior.
3. Lake Huron.
4. Lake Ontario.
5. Lake Michigan.

c. A list that completes a sentence

When a list is a grammatical part of the sentence, the items to be enumerated must belong to the same class, with a common idea introduced before the colon.

Writers can *keep the items within the text*: (1) by introducing the list with a colon; (2) by indenting all of each item and numbering each item; (3) by beginning each item with a lowercase letter; (4) by concluding each item but the last with a semicolon; (5) by placing a semicolon and "and" or "or" after the next-to-last item; and (6) by concluding the final item with a period unless the list does not conclude the textual sentence.

Or writers can choose to *separate that same list* with white space and an indented list:

1. by introducing the list with a colon;
2. by indenting all of each item and numbering each item;

3. by beginning each item with a lowercase letter;
4. by concluding each item but the last with a semicolon;
5. by placing a semicolon and “and” or “or” after the next-to-last item; and
6. by concluding the final item with a period (unless the list does not conclude the textual sentence).

Do not use a colon after a verb or a preposition.

A suspect has**:** no right to Miranda warnings before being searched.

A suspect has no right to Miranda warnings before being searched.

The police were nevertheless criticized for**:** arresting two soccer moms and taking them to the jail after police discovered one had a cake knife.

The police were nevertheless criticized for arresting two soccer moms and taking them to the jail after police discovered one had a cake knife.

Capitalization after a colon is optional, but most writers capitalize *complete* sentences after the colon and leave fragments in lowercase:

This has been a lesson for all neighborhood mothers**: d**o not take your cake knife to soccer practice.

This has been a lesson for all neighborhood mothers**: D**o not take your cake knife to soccer practice.

14. Punctuation ordinarily goes inside the quotation marks, except for colons and semicolons.

The car’s driver insisted, “We have been to a birthday party**.”**

The passenger reported that she had been terrified of the “flashing blue and red lights”**;** she is now under sedation.

15. Semicolons are necessary for a list that contains commas within a list of items. In these lists, you might think of the semicolons as monster commas.

The United States Supreme Court specifically rejected requiring police officers to advise detainees of the right to refuse consent; found such a warning impractical, if not too difficult to deliver; and concluded that the searches are a normal occurrence on streets, in offices, and in homes.

16. Use parentheses instead of commas when you would like to include information in a sentence but do not want to detract from the overall flow of the sentence. These parentheticals are sometimes less intrusive.

My mother (who is from an urban area in Germany) recently had problems when the doctor could not understand her accent.

The move (her third, in less than two years) proved very onerous.

SPECIFIC LEGAL WRITING RULES

17. Two complete sentences separated by a simple conjunction require a separating comma. (*and, or, nor, but, yet*)

This comma with a simple conjunction is not essential in other forms of writing like fiction**, but** legal writers depend on it to signal a new subject/verb and to help avoid confusion in legal analysis.

18. In technical (legal) writing, items in a series require commas between items and before the "and" or "or." (This is the serial or "Oxford" comma.)

The women had assumed people could get arrested only for breaking and entering, assault and battery and rape. (How many charges? Two or three?)

The women had assumed people could get arrested only for breaking and entering**,** assault and battery**, and** rape. (Three distinct, separate charges.)

19. In legal writing, a citation is treated as an interruptor (see #4 above) and requires commas both before and after the completed citation.

In the seminal case, *Schneckloth v. Bustamonte*, 412 U.S. 218, 231 (1973), the United States Supreme Court determined that there was a difference between voluntarily consenting to a search and being coerced into consenting to a search.

20. In legal writing, writers take special care to punctuate "that" and "which" as essential/nonessential clauses.

Federal authority **that requires informing** a suspect of his rights is derived through various United States Supreme Court cases, including *Miranda v. Arizona*, 384 U.S. 436 (1966).

Some federal statutes**, which include those related to income tax evasion,** require that an accused person is informed of all charges against him.

In the first example, the clause is essential to narrowing or *limiting* which authority is covered. In the second example, the clause helps only to *describe* which of "some" authority is covered; that authority isn't essential.

Notice that the essential clause does not have commas that punctuate the clause "out" of the main text. The clause is required there to establish meaning. Notice, too, that the nonessential clause *must* be punctuated out of the main text with *two commas*.

21. Legal writers must learn how to incorporate, punctuate, and indent quotations. Generally, *quotations* more than 49 words in length are block-indented, are single spaced, and do not have quotation marks around them.

The syllabus of *Miranda v. Arizona* states:

> [t]he atmosphere and environment of incommunicado interrogation as it exists today is inherently intimidating, and works to undermine the privilege against self-incrimination. Unless adequate preventive measures are taken to dispel the compulsion inherent in custodial surroundings, no statement obtained from the defendant can truly be the product of his free choice.

22. Ellipses and spacing indicate that you have omitted material from a passage being quoted. (A legal ellipsis mark is composed of three spaced periods.)

Aristotle once wrote that "[e]xcellence . . . is not an act but a habit."

A 1973 Supreme Court case set the standard by holding,[o]ne alternative . . . would be to advise him of that right before eliciting his consent. That . . . would be thoroughly impractical . . . . Consent searches are part of the standard investigatory techniques of law enforcement agencies. They normally occur on the highway, or in a person's home or office, and under informal and unstructured conditions.

Schneckloth v. Bustamante, 412 U.S. 218, 231–32 (1973).

23. Brackets signal a change in quoted material. Notice that you will add a period to the end of material if your syntax requires one.

You may make include some of the following changes to text within the brackets:

a) missing words or letters;

b) capitals changed to lowercase and lowercase words changed to capitals to fit your own sense of the quotation into your text;

c) additions that help explain ambiguous material in a quotation;

d) your own comments inserted into quoted material; and

e) the word "sic" to indicate an error repeated from the original ("sic" is a complete word meaning "in this manner" or "thus").

Following are examples of correctly placed brackets:

The women's defense was that their "weapon was only a **[**kitchen**]** knife used to cut birthday cakes."

"**[**S**]**ubject of a search does have the right to refuse consent to a search," reminded the court.

The inmate complained that his "direea **[sic]** had caused trouble for weeks."

What to Remember

- Choose punctuation marks that **help the reader** understand the substantive material. The marks are supposed to pull words together and push them apart appropriately.
- **Review** the **general** punctuation list.
- Learn those marks required specifically for legal writers.
- Check **Bluebook/ALWD manuals** to ensure your marks conform to expected legal form and format.

CONCLUDING EXERCISE

The answers to the Concluding Exercise can be found on page 99.

Try these concluding quizzes that mix the punctuation rules you have just reviewed.

1. In Dallas a 16 year old kid with a glossy-red convertible was stopped for speeding.

2. He pulled over to the side of the road. And was so nervous he hit the curb.

3. "Ohmygod no", the policeman heard him chanting.

4. "This will be an easy stop," the policeman said into his car speaker; "because he is already admitting he's in trouble."

5. First the policeman walked completely around the car, noting its condition, stopped by the passenger window and asked to see the boy's driver's license.

6. He asked for information—the driver's name, owner of the vehicle, where the driver was going, and if he knew he was exceeding the speed limit.

7. The police officer said,

> "You have the right to refuse to answer these simple questions, but I advise you to answer them and clear up any confusion now."

8. When the boy quickly spouted the answers the police officer wrote several of them down, and grunted at the rest.

9. The process needed to go quickly which the officer knew from experience.

10. Some speeders will become indignant and argumentative and some will be embarrassed and just want to sign the forms and leave.

♦♦♦♦

Only as we tumble our words onto the page or into a dictating machine do we begin to see our story, our argument, take shape. The time to focus on the relationships between the disparate parts of our document is during the reading of the first draft. Only then can we see that point one is independent of point two, but that points three and four are inexorably tied to the outcome of point two and thus dependent.

Terri LeClercq, Expert Legal Writing 60 (1995).

♦♦♦♦

5

ORGANIZING WITH STYLE

An undergraduate paper and a legal memorandum or brief share many elements of good writing. You may have learned in undergraduate school that good writing requires a particular organization: a topic paragraph that indicates to the reader what will be happening in the paper, good paragraphs dedicated to the major themes outlined in your introductory section, solid paragraphs that are easy to follow and contain limited information introduced by a topic sentence or appropriate transition, and a conclusion that advances or sums of the theme of the paper.

Legal Writing is no different, but may seem very different at first, partially because the object of legal writing is not to opine on your brilliance and demonstrate your immense (and varied) vocabulary, but to analyze cases and apply them in ways that will solve legal problems in an analytical manner.

Legal readers have been trained to expect a specific order of information, so this chapter helps you to adjust to those expectations. This new organization is at first frustrating, so you might have one of at least two responses: (1) you can bang your head on the desk and insist to your professor that he simply doesn't understand your brilliant analysis, or (2) you can read the chapters in your legal-analysis text and also this chapter, take a deep breath, and follow the formula. Remind yourself that you have come to law school to learn this different organization. Mastering this organization will be one of the first important lessons of law school.

UNDERGRADUATE VERSUS LAW SCHOOL ORGANIZATION

You will be introduced to various formats of legal writing in law school, but two primary types of documents will be those focusing on objective analysis (e.g., the Memorandum of Law) and those focusing on persuasive advocacy (e.g., a Motion). The Memorandum of Law is an objective document that explains the law from both sides of an issue. Advocacy documents are persuasive documents filed with a court. An advocacy document uses the law as a basis to argue a legal position with the court. These documents are slightly different from each other and certainly different in tone; however, all legal documents share various organizational qualities. For purposes of explanation, this chapter will use the Memorandum of Law as the example of legal organization.

Legal organization differs from general undergraduate organization in several important ways: you will find it more formulaic, more repetitive, and more dependent on sources than on flashes of insight. Nonetheless, you will quickly realize that an undergraduate paper and a legal paper share many elements of good writing.

Below is an undergraduate paper with its elements labeled on the left side in familiar terminology. To the right is the new terminology that you might apply for those same elements, plus terminology for the new and different elements that you will be required to include when writing in law school. Try to focus on how the familiar organization of the undergraduate paper will parallel what will be the organization of a legal paper.

Undergraduate		**Legal**
Essay "**title**" will reflect its contents. ➧	**Legal Responsibility for Binge Drinking at Fraternity-Sponsored Parties**	➧ "**Memorandum of Law**" (or "Memo" or something similar)
Background. ➧ Note the beginning "hook" intended to draw the reader in.	It is no secret that binge drinking is a major problem on college campuses. Binge drinking has been responsible for many campus deaths within the last decade. Forty-two percent of college students report having indulged in binge drinking. The majority of binge drinking occurs during parties, especially parties organized by fraternities. This essay will examine the current	➧ **Background information setting up legal issue.** Usually contained in a Statement of Facts and is not intended to draw the reader in as would be done in a typical essay.

Thesis. Sentence anticipates organization ("both sides") and conclusion ("best solution").

state of the law concerning whether fraternities should be held responsible for injuries related to binge drinking. It will also suggest ways in which fraternities can avoid getting sued.

Description of what the remainder of the writing is about. This is ordinarily the current status of the legal proceeding.

Topic Sentence.

Development of paragraph thesis.

Introduction of next sub-thesis.

Responsibility for providing alcohol to others is divided into two main categories. The first is for bar owners and bartenders. The second is for others who provide alcohol to others, such as those who hold a party. A person who holds a party and serves alcohol may be sued if guests get drunk and injure others. This is called "Social Host Liability." Whether a person owns a bar or holds a party, two main rules apply. First, alcohol may not be given to a minor. Second, alcohol may not be given to a "visibly intoxicated person." Bar owners and bartenders are held to a higher standard than others because people working in a bar are expected to be on the look-out for a minor, or to be able to recognize a person who's been drinking a lot.

Main thesis statement or general rule of law.

Elaborations of the rule. (Would include case citations in a final memo.)

Additional sub-thesis related to the general rule of law.

Further explanation of sub-thesis.

Topic sentence.

Both sides of the issue.

The responsibility for a fraternity hosting a party falls into the category of Social Host Liability. A fraternity could be held responsible for injuries caused to binge drinkers, or for injuries caused to others by binge drinkers if it can be shown that alcohol was made available to minors or alcohol was given to someone already drunk. Although a fraternity would not be held to as high a standard as a bar owner, it would be easy to prove whether alcohol was given to a minor or to a drunk person, especially if binge drinking was going on at the party.

Topic sentence. Sentence contains an **application of the rules** of law to fraternities. It is followed by the application of "elaborations" from the more general rule of law.

Counterposition related to how to disprove liability.

Conclusion. ➧ Partial repeat of thesis is. Words of wisdom and advice.

Fraternities must take care to make sure that they are not encouraging either underage or binge drinking. Those who attend college fraternity parties must be closely monitored to make sure that alcohol is not accessible to minors and that binge drinking does not occur. This would be the right thing to do to keep college students safe, and also to prevent law suits brought against fraternities for the parties they host.

➧**Overall Conclusion.** Includes suggestions for a potential course of conduct.

However, as similar as "good" writing may be from discipline to discipline, there are important, but sometimes subtle, differences between undergraduate writing and legal writing. This chart might be useful in highlighting some of those differences.

Undergraduate Papers	**Legal Memoranda**
GOALS **Deductively move from big picture with specific examples** • prove **research** • show spark of **imagination** or innovation • general **resolution/** recommendation	***GOALS*** **Inductively synthesize elements of cases while presenting research both deductively and inductively** • **answer** specific legal question • **apply Rule** (statute/cases) to client's facts • address **both sides** of the issue • conclude with **likely outcome**
INTRODUCTION • A hook to **interest** the reader in the topic. • general **history** or background of topic • **thesis**, usually last sentence	***INTRODUCTION*** • **Rule** to be examined • **Exceptions or elaborations** related to the general rule • **Application** of client's **facts** • **Conclusion** or prediction regarding outcome of legal question

STRUCTURE • follows **thesis** • needs **topic sentences** to support thesis • needs **transitions** to connect major sections and to connect sentences • often focuses on **writer's ideas** about material rather than on deriving an answer to a question	***STRUCTURE*** variation of **IRAC** but will always include • the **Rule** being examined (this may be a subpart of an overarching general rule) • a "synthesis" and explanation of pertinent **cases** that have analyzed the Rule • an **application** that compares and contrasts the cases' facts with the current client's facts • **counter-analysis** that anticipates what the other side will argue differently • **refutation** of any counter-interpretation; and • a **Conclusion** for each point
SUPPORTING AUTHORITY • **primary material and supplemental authority** (this differs from paper to paper; for instance, if writing about a work of literature, the primary material would be the literature, while supplemental authority would include critiques and commentaries)	***SUPPORTING AUTHORITY*** • **always focuses on statutes and cases with specific reference to jurisdictions and years of decision** • may occasionally allow for secondary sources such as law reviews or restatements, but these are considered unacceptable as primary authority
CONCLUSION • **brief repetition** of contents of paper and conclusion • a **general resolution** to problem/issue raised • perhaps a **spark of imagination** or innovative suggestion	***CONCLUSION*** • **review** of law previously articulated • summary of ways court could apply the **law and major arguments** that might be made • **prediction** of how court will view pertinent law and perhaps suggestion for next step in legal process

OVERALL STYLE	***OVERALL STYLE***
• tendency toward longer topic sentences • tendency toward varying language • tendency toward being more implicit than explicit • tendency toward expressing author's commentary as opposed to providing straightforward answers to questions posed	• topic sentences short and to the point • language deliberately repetitive • prose that is succinct and explicit • author's opinions about the law, but only author's opinions as to how a court may interpret the law based on the existing law

Now let's take a look at how these differences play out when we transform the undergraduate paper, above, into a legal memorandum. Pay close attention to what has been removed and added to an undergraduate paper as we transform the paper into memo form. Also, keep in mind that this memo does not include the legal citations that are mandatory in a legal memo. Finally, keep in mind that, similar to essay writing, all memos are not created equally. As formulaic as legal writing is, there is not a definitive number of cases or paragraphs required. Although the overall structure always remains the same, there are variations in legal writing, just as there are in essay writing.

MEMO

► **Title of Document.**

TO: Karin Mika
FROM: Student 4500
DATE: April 30, 2015
RE: Liability of Fraternity when person who was binge drinking falls from balcony.

► **Heading information, typical in a law office and in first-year Legal Writing courses**

Statement of Facts

► **Specific background information is included in the Statement of Facts. The facts replace the opening paragraph of the essay and do not attempt to "hook" the reader.**

On March 21, 2015, the Alpha Zeta fraternity held a party to celebrate spring break. A 21-year-old junior, Steven Johnson, attended the party. Various witnesses testified that Johnson engaged in "binge drinking" during the party and that the fraternity provided the alcohol and encouraged the binge drinking, even after Johnson was obviously drunk. At some time between midnight and 1 a.m., Johnson went upstairs to a room or roof in the fraternity house and apparently fell two floors to the ground. He suffered a broken leg and broken ribs. Johnson has since sued the fraternity for negligence, alleging that the fraternity is responsible for encouraging him to binge drink, and that his drunkenness caused him to fall from the roof. This memo is being submitted to examine the issue of whether a fraternity is liable for injuries related to serving alcohol at parties,

► **Information anticipates the memo's contents and why it is being written: to answer legal questions. Memos are not written to discuss general, interesting issues.**

and, in particular, liable for injuries occurring as the result of binge drinking.

Issue

WHETHER A FRATERNITY THAT SPONSORS A PARTY, PROVIDES ALCOHOL TO THE ATTENDEES, AND ENCOURAGES BINGE DRINKING IS RESPONSIBLE FOR INJURIES SUSTAINED BY A 21-YEAR-OLD STUDENT WHO ATTENDED THE PARTY WHEN THAT INDIVIDUAL HAD BEEN BINGE DRINKING AND LATER FELL OFF THE ROOF OF THE FRATERNITY HOUSE.

► **The legal issue is a formulaic segment that sets out both the legal question that is being asked and the pertinent facts that would lead to the resolution of the legal issue. It is traditionally set out in all capital letters, but not always. There is no counterpart for the Issue in an essay.**

The general rule is that a fraternity may be responsible for injuries sustained as the result of drinking or binge drinking that occurs during fraternity-sponsored parties. Responsibility for providing alcohol to others is divided into two main categories. The first is for bar owners and bartenders. The second is for anyone who provides alcohol to others, such as when they hold a party. A person who holds a party and serves alcohol may be sued if guests get drunk and injure themselves or others. This is called "Social Host Liability." Whether a person owns a bar or holds a party, two main rules apply. First, alcohol may not be given to a minor. Second, alcohol may not be given to a "visibly intoxicated person." The law holds bar owners and bartenders to a higher standard than others because people working in a bar are expected to be on the look-out for a minor, or to be able to recognize a person who's been drinking a lot.

► **Introductory Segment. This is actually a short answer and is composed of the general rule of law; any specific additional material the reader might need to know about the most general rule; application of the law to the legal issue; and a prediction for the litigation (e.g., "would the court find that a cause of action exists?"). The actual introduction <u>will have citations</u> following each legal principle.**

Several cases demonstrate how the law defines Social Host Liability. In *Morris v. Arthur*, the court held that a person holding a graduation party was not liable for the injuries suffered by a person who, when drunk, jumped into the shallow end of the family pool. The court reasoned that there was no evidence the host of the party provided any alcohol. Similarly, in *Montenegro v. Nyland*, the court also held that an individual holding a party was not liable for an accident caused by a drunken individual who had been at the party. According to the court, the person who had attended the party had already been drunk when he had arrived and was someone who had just shown up at what became a very large party.

► **Topic sentence.**

► **Legal authority to be used in analyzing the legal issue presented. In legal writing, the legal authority must be explicitly stated for a later logical comparison. This is different from essay writing where the authority for a premise often is implicit or appears after the point has been made. In legal writing, cases or statutes almost always appear *before***

Conversely, in *Morrison v. Phi Beta Kappa*, the court held that a fraternity was responsible for injuries caused by a person who left a fraternity party drunk and caused an automobile accident. There, evidence demonstrated that the person causing the accident was served alcohol at a party by a bartender who was a member of the fraternity's board. Further evidence demonstrated that the student in question was served alcohol long after he was unable to communicate coherently and yet no one from the fraternity questioned whether he would be driving home after the party.

the writer makes a point based on that authority.

These cases suggest that the Alpha Zeta fraternity will be held responsible for the injuries to Steve Johnson. Social Hosts may be held liable for injuries caused by those intoxicated if it is demonstrated that the host served alcohol to someone who is already intoxicated. In *Morrison* specifically, the court held the fraternity responsible because evidence suggested that the fraternity had "control" over the serving of alcohol and did not monitor what happened to an intoxicated person after he left the party. Here, similarly, evidence indicates that it was the fraternity itself that encouraged Johnson's binge drinking and did not monitor what he did after he was obviously drunk. This similarity may cause a court to conclude that the Alpha Zeta fraternity should be responsible for the injuries to Johnson.

- **Topic sentence in which the writer informs the reader that analysis of the cases will begin. The topic sentence also acts like a mini conclusion.**
- **In structured legal analysis, cases introduced previously are the basis of comparison to the issue being analyzed. Note: The premise introduced previously is repeated before the analogy is made.**

However, the defendant fraternity may assert that it had little control over what the plaintiff did at the party and thus should have no legal liability for his injuries. For instance, in *Montenegro*, the court found there was no liability because there was evidence that the plaintiff was already drunk when he arrived at the party, and that he was just one guest at a very large party. Alpha Zeta fraternity may assert that, based on the rationale of *Montenegro*, it could not possibly control the actions of all the attendees and thus should not be held liable for what happened to them.

- **Counterposition. Note: A legal premise from one of the cases mentioned previously is set out before the actual counterposition is articulated.**

A court is unlikely to find Alpha Zeta's argument has merit. In cases involving Social Host Liability, the court tends to focus on two factors: control of the alcohol and encouraging the continuation of drinking. In the case involving Johnson, those in charge of Alpha Zeta fraternity not only provided the alcohol but also encouraged the binge drinking. This situation is more similar to what occurred in *Morrison*. Thus, the court is likely to find that the Social Host defendant had responsibility to ensure that the plaintiff did not injure himself or others.

- **Refutation. Again, a case premise is set out before an analogy is made. Note: In each of the three analysis paragraphs, the final sentence acts as a wrap-up for the comparison/contrast being made.**

Conclusion

The general rule is that a social host may be held responsible for injuries caused by intoxicated persons who are served alcohol when those individuals are "visibly

- **Conclusion that repeats the basic premises of law, highlights the major positions, and reflects on what a court is likely to do.**

intoxicated." In finding liability, courts tend to focus on whether the host of the party was in control of providing the alcohol to guests and encouraged their drinking. Here, the facts indicate that the defendant fraternity provided alcohol to the plaintiff and encouraged binge drinking. As a result, it is likely a court will find the fraternity responsible for the injuries suffered by the plaintiff when he fell from the roof.

HOW TO BEGIN TO ORGANIZE

The crux of writing any type of legal document is doing research related to an issue the client has confronted. You'll learn about the client's issue from the client's facts, or the client's story. Your resulting legal document will analyze the law in relation to the client's story to help the client come up with some legal resolution.

Thus, you must first gather information (do legal research) so that you'll be able to understand the law. This is sometimes easier said than done because novice legal researchers do not always know what they are looking for. Nonetheless, you cannot begin writing about a topic until you understand the issues. Consequently, your research phase in the first year of law school is likely going to be longer than the research phase in undergraduate school where you were probably comfortable with the knowledge you had in your field of study after a few years. Moreover, the complexity of the research phase, combined with the formulaic nature of legal writing, translates into a writing process that is quite different from what occurred in undergraduate school. Until you full understand the nature of the structure of legal analysis, it is impossible to write a paper in a few hours. Rather, you'll develop the paper over time, combining your understanding of the material with the appropriate strategy you'll need for that material.

Each person who has been a successful writer organizes differently. Some begin with an outline that is filled in as research develops. Some learn by writing and thus write down everything they know; then they later bring coherent organization to the document through a continuous editing process. Others simply have an internalized organization and thus begin to write a nearly finished document soon after they have some mastery of the material. (Do not judge your progress against these particular writers.)

No matter what your methodology for organization, some constants make legal writing coherent. As a novice legal writer, you should always have these organizational components in mind as you begin to research a particular legal issue.

Introductory Material

No doubt all students entering law school have been well trained in writing thesis or introductory paragraphs. A college thesis paragraph, as indicated in the example above, usually starts with a "hook" to lure the reader to read further, encompasses the theme of the paper, and provides the reader with a road map of what the paper or essay will do. The introductory paragraph of a legal memorandum is, in many respects, the same as a thesis paragraph—and yet very different.

Keep in mind the function of a legal memorandum—its intent is to answer a question presented as succinctly and accurately as possible. Lawyers are very busy people. They need the information in a hurry, and they don't want or expect excess explanation. There is no need to lure the reader to read onward, nor is there a need for any historical backdrop as to how the law became what it now is. Thus, in writing an introduction, the legal writer's job is to distill the law from perhaps hundreds of cases into two or three sentences and give the reader a short summary that answers the reader's original question. In doing so, the introductory segment also provides the "set-up" for the remainder of the document in the same way that a thesis road map would do. The introduction should guide the reader to the essential legal components in the paper.

OTHER COMPONENTS OF ORGANIZING WITH STYLE

Using Headings as Signposts

Long documents *require* headings; shorter documents are sometimes *aided* by them. In either case, your readers will benefit from the quick overview of the larger picture in your thesis and setup, and they can then skim your headings. As a writer, you will also benefit when you take time to summarize the paragraphs' contents as headings: if the headings in your first draft don't summarize your discussion when you skim them, or if the headings bounce you around from one idea to another, you are now on alert to make the necessary adjustments to your draft.

Before using headings, you obviously must understand what you are trying to achieve. Headings that separate out only small chunks of information can be distracting. Additionally, headings should not be used to replace topic sentences of paragraphs. They act independently as a guide to the reader. A bonus for careful writers is the visual effect of headings: readers can be pulled by the headings and subheadings to the section of specific interest. Here are a few other suggestions you should consider as you develop your headings:

1. Headings need to **satisfy the reader's needs.** Headings labeled "Element One," "Element Two," and "Element Three" do no satisfy anything. Instead, a heading should summarize the material within that block of text.

2. Headings should **reflect the setup.** If, after a setup that announces three elements of negligence, you insert a major heading to introduce the first element of negligence but do not use headings for the following two, your reader won't understand that those three elements are parallel.

3. Headings should **be consistent in content, grammatical structure, and typography.** If the first major heading is a full sentence, then all the other major headings should be full sentences. Similarly, the subheadings may be only phrases, but then each subheading should be a phrase. If major subheadings are flush left and in bold face, then sub-headings need to be differentiated as a group by a consistent indent, or they should be in italics.

4. Headings should be **independent of the text** that follows them. Your paragraphs should begin with topic headings that label and introduce the material that follows.

5. Headings should not be a mere **repetition** of the topic sentence of the paragraph that follows. A topic sentence will probably contain more words, and thus more detail, than a heading has. The material following a heading should logically flow from the heading, but a complete mimicry of the heading would be redundant and likely disconcerting for the reader.

Using Topic Sentences and Transitions Effectively

Topic sentences work in much the same way as a thesis: they introduce the idea within the paragraph; they set boundaries for the paragraph; and they help tie ideas together. Reexamine the student essay above, noticing that each paragraph from a carefully constructed undergraduate paper contains a topic sentence that introduced or summarized the paragraph's content. That's a convention that remains in legal writing.

Experiment with your own rough drafts by separating each topic sentence from your text: is each one a strong introduction to, or conclusion about, that paragraph's main idea? Next, examine the coherence of the topic sentences as they relate to the overall setup. At this point, you may decide that some added transitions will smooth the reader's path.

Take, for example, the following paragraph, which is a variation extracted from the memo earlier in the chapter:

In *Morris v. Arthur*, the court held that a person holding a graduation party was not liable for the injuries suffered by a person who, when drunk, jumped into the shallow end of the family pool. The court reasoned that there was no evidence the host of the party provided any alcohol. In *Montenegro v. Nyland*, the court also held that an individual holding a party was not liable for an accident caused by a drunken individual who had been at the party. According to the court, the person who had attended the party had already been drunk when he had arrived, and was someone who had just shown up at what became a very large party. Finally, in *Morrison v. Phi Beta Kappa*, the court held that a fraternity was responsible for injuries caused by a person who left a fraternity party drunk and caused an automobile accident. There, evidence demonstrated that the person causing the accident was served alcohol at the party by a bartender who was a member of the fraternity's board. Further evidence demonstrated that the student in question was served alcohol long after he was unable to communicate coherently and that no one from the fraternity questioned whether he would be driving home after the party.

Without a topic sentence, the "paragraph" is nothing more than a bunch of sentences about what seem to be similar cases. The reader is left to guess the context for the cases, and even to guess how the cases fit into the main theme of the paper. The reader might guess correctly, but the reader might also guess incorrectly. Your job is to make sure that there is no guesswork on behalf of the reader.

Transitions perform the similar function of highlighting what the writer intends to say; they provide for logical connections between the sentences of the paragraphs. Transitions can be used to tie themes of paragraphs together, separate themes of paragraphs, or tie sentences together within paragraphs. Without appropriate transitions, the reader may be left to wander or even be hopelessly confused.

Consider the following paragraph:

There are several reasons why the rationale of *Texas v. Johnson* supports the position that Plaintiff's First Amendment rights were violated. Similar to the situation in *Johnson*, the Plaintiff's shirt represented a commonly recognized political symbol—the president of the United States. Finally, the president's face was enveloped in the colors of the American flag, colors dubbed by the *Johnson* Court as "symbolic of nationhood" and America itself. Subsequently, the shirt was worn soon after the President's inauguration. This context, similar to the context considered by the *Johnson* Court, demonstrated that plaintiff's intended message in support of the President and increased the likelihood that those viewing the shirt would understand this intent.

Note that the paragraph does start with a topic sentence that presumably also acts as a transition; however, the internal transitions send the reader in all kinds of different and unintended directions. By the time the reader has finished the paragraph, the reader has no idea that the paragraph actually does make a pretty decent argument. Compare:

> There are several reasons why the rationale of *Texas v. Johnson* supports the position that Plaintiff's First Amendment rights were violated. **First,** similar to the situation in *Johnson*, the Plaintiff's shirt represented a commonly recognized political symbol—the president of the United States. **Second,** the president's face was enveloped in the colors of the American flag, colors dubbed by the *Johnson* Court as "symbolic of nationhood" and America itself. **Moreover,** the shirt was worn soon after the president's inauguration. This context, similar to the context considered by the *Johnson* Court, demonstrated the plaintiff's intended message in support of the president; it increased the likelihood that those viewing the shirt would understand this intent.

Examine the undergraduate paper again, this time for **transitions**, and where you might have added them if this were your draft. The idea that those little transitions are important is a strange one, and yet they perform a critical function in connecting ideas. Whether connecting large-scale segments, paragraphs, sentences, or words, transitions signal relationships, and relationships signal clarity. Thus, without topic sentences and transitions, no paragraph makes sense. It is just a series of ideas loosely connected in a way that must be assumed by the reader. The omission forces the reader to do your thinking for you. The omission can create frustration on the part of your reader (your boss, court personnel, your client).

OTHER HELPFUL ADVICE FOR ORGANIZING WITH STYLE

Here are a few additional tips for guiding your reader and making sure that your writing is as clear as possible. Note that a couple of these are applicable to all forms of writing, while a few are specific for legal writing.

1. Use **verb tenses** correctly and effectively.

Verb tenses should be kept consistent within the framework of a paragraph or segment of a paper. Traditionally, the law exists in the present tense, while the facts of cases and court holdings are conveyed in the past tense. Thus, it is appropriate to say, "The Fourth Amendment *protects* the citizenry from unreasonable searches and seizures" (indeed, it would be rather strange to read that the Fourth Amendment apparently once *protected* the citizenry from unreasonable searches and seizures). It isn't appropriate to say, "In *Morrison*, the court notes that the defendant is a person who is walking on the darkened street in a crime-ridden neighborhood." (The proper phrasing should be, "The court *noted* . . . .)

Occasionally using the present verb tense can be appropriate, such as when a court states a general proposition using the facts from a case. For instance, "In *Morrison*, the court notes that a person walking down a darkened street in a crime-ridden neighborhood is someone who might be deemed suspicious." However, you should take care to describe facts that occurred in the past as having occurred in the past rather than as a blow-by-blow description as would be given by a sportscaster.

A different type of problem occurs when the writer shifts verb tenses within a paragraph or within a sentence. That's not to say that sometimes verb tenses can't be shifted appropriately in some circumstances (e.g., "In finding the defendant *was* lawfully *detained*, the court first *acknowledged* that the Fourth Amendment ***protects*** the citizenry from unreasonable searches and seizures."). Nonetheless, verb tense shifts can be tricky and can make a piece of writing really nonsensical.

> In *Morrison*, the court holds that the Fourth Amendment was not violated. *Morrison* deals with an individual who is walking down a street. The street is dark and was in a crime-ridden neighborhood. The defendant looks suspicious. The court ruled that the Fourth Amendment is not violated because the officers have reasonable cause to detain the defendant.

Note how the reader is forced to focus on the constantly shifting verb tenses rather than on the actual content of the paragraph.

Compare:

> In *Morrison*, the court held that the Fourth Amendment was not violated. *Morrison* dealt with an individual who was walking down a street. The street was dark and was in a crime-ridden neighborhood. Additionally, the defendant looked suspicious. The court ruled that the Fourth Amendment was not violated because the officers had reasonable cause to detain the defendant.

2. Use **repetition** of words/ideas and **dovetailing**[5] (linking material from the end of one sentence to the beginning of the next) to create cohesion within the document and to help readers understand your legal analysis.

---

[5] For a detailed discussion on dovetailing, *see* Oates & Enquist, THE LEGAL WRITING HANDBOOK: ANALYSIS RESEARCH & WRITING (6th ed. Wolters Kluwer Law & Business 2014).

Earlier, we mentioned the concept of **dovetailing** as a method of leading the reader through your written material. **Repetition** and **dovetailing** are also beneficial tools for constructing clear legal analysis.

Compare the following examples:

a. Based on the case of *Omnibus*, it is unlikely that the University will succeed in its cause of action for trespass to chattels. An interference or intermeddling with the property of another without permission is an actionable tort. This disturbance or hindrance must cause some type of damage to the property that might be owned. In *Omnibus*, the court determined that no harm existed because the plaintiff had use of a fax machine for a substantial amount of time. It may be argued that the University was not deprived of its network at any stage of the month in question. Thus, no actionable deprivation occurred.

b. Based on the case of *Omnibus*, it is unlikely the University will succeed in its cause of action for *trespass to chattels*. A **trespass to chattels** occurs when there is an unauthorized *interference or intermeddling* with the *property of another*. This **interference or intermeddling** must cause some type of *harm or damage* to the **property of another**. In *Omnibus*, the court determined that no **harm or damage** existed because the plaintiff was not *deprived* of its fax machine for a *substantial amount of time*. Similarly, it may be argued that the University was not **deprived** of its network for any **length of time**. Thus, there was neither **harm nor damage**.

Which of these paragraphs is easier to follow? Correct, the **dovetailing** and **repetition** in the second example make the writer's points blend together much better than the first example.

3. Avoid being **overly creative** in constructing legal documents.

Legal writing is often regarded as "dry." Although this book is all about how to make your legal writing more stylish, we acknowledge you can't turn on your inner creative muse just to add stylistic verve.

Consider this beginning for a statement of facts for a memo:

It was a dark and stormy night. The defendant, 18 years old, scared and alone in one of the most dangerous areas of the city, found himself without transportation after the water pump of his 1980 Honda Civic exploded without warning. The date was April 28, 2014, a Friday. The defendant had previously been employed as a truck driver.

It was within these ranks that he met several unsavory characters. It was these characters that introduced him to the verboten world of drugs, and it was drugs that caused his downfall on that evening when Officer Jose Felipe, a 20-year veteran of the Metropolitan Police Department, saw him walking down the street.

Perhaps if this were a novel, these facts could be appropriate (if rather clichéd). But for a memo, the facts need to be more concise, logically arranged, and more to the "legal" point:

On April 28, 2014, the defendant was arrested for possession of drugs. On that evening, the defendant was walking down 36th Street. He had left his vehicle after it broke down. The defendant was attempting to find a telephone to call for help when he was spotted walking down the street by Officer Jose Felipe, a 20-year veteran of the Metropolitan Police Department.

Thus, the moral of the story is what the moral of the story always is: **write for your audience!**

Although this chapter has focused on the expected organization for legal writing, keep in mind that there are some variances to the way a document is organized. There is not always a right or a wrong way to organize. Your Legal Writing professor will teach you about jurisdictional hierarchy, but sometimes there is not an exactly "right" case that must appear first in the document you are writing, nor an exactly "right" sentence that must be the beginning of your document. True, there are constants in legal writing, but both the audience and the message determine effective organization.

Here's a useful tip for examining the organization of your draft: cut the draft into paragraph blocks, scramble the blocks, and reassemble them to their original order using only topic sentences and transitions. If you have to reread the full contents of each of your own paragraphs to recognize their content, imagine how difficult it would be for your reader to follow what you are saying! Better return to the draft and sharpen your internal cues.

What to Remember

- Be able to **recognize the components** for the legal memorandum **and the logical structure** of legal analysis.
- Use **headings** to signal content.
- **Create topic sentences** that anticipate each paragraph's content.
- **Add transitions** to connect major sections and paragraphs.
- Make the document cohesive and easy to read by using **repetition and dovetailing**.
- Use **appropriate verb tenses** to convey the substance of your material.
- Avoid being **overly creative** in legal writing.

CONCLUDING EXERCISE

The answers to the Concluding Exercise can be found on page 100.

1. **Introductory paragraphs.** How might this first introductory paragraph be re-written so that it follows the legal format of setting out rules and their definitions before applying the facts of a case?

   Exercise 1:

   Because the letters "FU" are commonly understood as shorthand for a sexual phrase, it is likely that a court would find the plaintiff's requested license plate offensive. The standard used to assess offensiveness is the "reasonable person who understands the language [being used]." Courts have interpreted a combination of letters as offensive if they have a sexual connotation, if they suggest a derogatory meaning, or if they are insulting to a certain segment of the population. The non-offensive intent of the person using the phrase/letters in question is irrelevant. As a result, it is likely that the plaintiff will be denied the right to have the ILVTOFU license plate. It is irrelevant that the plaintiff did not intend to convey a derogatory meaning. In

California, a person who chooses what is considered an offensive combination of letters for a personalized license plate may be denied the opportunity to have that plate.

2. **Headings.** List section or paragraph headings that might follow the introductory segment below:

Exercise 2:

Conduct is protected by the First Amendment if it amounts to speech. Conduct amounts to speech when there is intent to convey a particular message and when there is a great likelihood that the message would be understood by those who viewed it. Intent to convey a particular message exists where the message can be determined objectively. Additionally, even if the courts have considered certain conduct protected, a high school may prohibit it if the school believes that the conduct will result in a disruption to the learning environment.

Although the Plaintiff wore a Hillary Clinton t-shirt, it is unclear what his message was in wearing the shirt and unclear what message was received by those who viewed the t-shirt. As a result, it is not likely the court would consider the wearing of the shirt protected speech. Even if the wearing of the shirt is considered protected speech, the school experienced a history of disruptions resulting from students wearing celebrity t-shirts. As a result, it is likely the court will find the school was within its rights to ask the plaintiff to turn his Hillary Clinton t-shirt inside out.

3. **Headings (2).** Read the following introductory material and then assess the headings that follow. First, are these headings appropriate? Second, if not, how can they be improved? (Assume a defendant wishes to challenge the admissibility of evidence discovered by a drug-sniff dog named Miley whose service record is less than stellar.)

Exercise 3:

The Fourth Amendment to the United States Constitution guarantees "[t]he right of the people to be secure . . . against unreasonable searches and seizures." A canine's sniff of luggage in a public place by a narcotics detection dog is not considered a "search" in and of itself. However, the canine sniff must be "sufficiently reliable" in order to establish probable cause. Sufficient reliability is generally present if the dog is "well-trained." Although there is no bright-line test for establishing "well-trained," courts have generally looked at two factors: records of the canine's successes and failures during certification training, and records of false alerts after training.

Given the general rule and cited case law, it appears that the evidence uncovered by the search at issue should be suppressed. First, it appears that Miley is not an adequately trained canine. As the facts indicate, Miley's certification was received only after two previous failed attempts. In addition, Miley made a number of false alerts after attaining certification. Accordingly, the totality of the circumstances surrounding Miley's certification and field records lead to a reasonable conclusion that Miley was neither "well-trained" nor "sufficiently reliable" and thus probable cause was not present. As a result, it is likely that a court will suppress the evidence obtained from the defendant.

1. A canine drug sniff dog must be sufficiently reliable.
2. There are two factors a court looks at in determining whether a dog is well-trained.
3. Certification standards.

4. Topic Sentence, Transitions, and Dovetailing. Add appropriate material to help readers follow this discussion.

Exercise 4:

The court determined that a police officer could conduct a search only if it was reasonably believed that the defendant was carrying contraband. The court determined that a stop could be made if the police officer believed a defendant looked suspicious. The court determined that an officer could look at various factors, including whether the neighborhood was generally crime-ridden and whether the defendant looked out-of-place or was attempting to evade police.

5. Verb Tense. Review this paragraph and revise the verb tenses.

Exercise 5:

In general, the law was that the First Amendment protects freedom of speech and expression. In the Supreme Court case of *Tinker*, the Court considers whether wearing black armbands (to protest the Vietnam War) is protected in a school. In reaching its decision, the Court concluded that the school has the right to restrict some forms of personal expression, but not the wearing of the armbands. The Court further states that, prior to restricting expression, the school fails to present evidence that the restricted expression might have caused unrest.

The Daily N

Sunday, August 30, 2015

Senior Neutering – for free!

Because of the popularity of the program last year in which senior residents of Austin could have all recently adopted shelter pets spayed and neutered for free, the city is again offering the service in 2016.

Last year, Pets 4Ever held an adoption drive sponsored by the Getman Veterinary Clinic. Each pet adopted during the drive by anyone over the age of 55 was able to have the pet spayed or neutered for free. The Clinic also provided a free checkup for all animals and discount coupons for vaccines. The event was such a success that the Getman Veterinary Clinic has offered to sponsor the event once more.

The opportunity to adopt will take place at all Pets 4Ever locations during the weekend of April 15-17, 2016.

Re
foll
imp

The
that
rela
the
beh
of a
exp
in l
its
beh
con
or v

♦ ♦ ♦ ♦

The secret of [writing] is never to put more on a given page than the common reader can lap off it with no strain whatsoever on his habitually slack attention.

Ezra Pound

♦ ♦ ♦ ♦

6

PRESENTING MATERIAL WITH STYLE

Remember the advice in the *Message to Students*: your readers are not going to read your document because they have extra time or because they need entertainment. Rather, they need information—and fast. To help them find that information, writers should make each document as attractive and accessible as possible.

The popularity of the Internet demonstrates that most people prefer receiving their information along with some type of visual component and expect the information to be gained quickly and easily. Television demonstrates the same. Many a marketing consultant has made a living trying to anticipate just what you would like to "see" so that you will purchase a product or watch a particular newscaster.

The need for order and neatness in appearance is nothing new. Imagine that you decide to purchase a new car. You enter the car lot, and there are two identical cars sitting next to each other. One is shiny and polished; the other is caked in mud. How many of you would honestly say that you prefer the car that is caked in mud?

So, too, is the preference of the readers of written documents. Two documents may have identical content, but the reader will always prefer the document that is well-proofread, visually appealing, and neatly put together.

Why is that?

Despite the fact that not all of us are equally organized and tidy, all of us do crave some type of organization in our lives. It is what makes us adjust pictures that are askew on a wall or what distracts us if something is out of place in our daily routines.

A pleasing presentation is even more important when you deal with legal writing and legal readers. Legal readers read quickly. They expect content in a certain order and expect not to be distracted during their reading. These distractions can be misused words, headings that do not match the material that follows them, legal concepts that are out of order, incorrect citations, typographical errors and misspelled words, or presentation that is simply not neat and orderly.

As a legal writer, you might not always be able to produce content as amazing as you would like. Sometimes your efforts may be hindered by time constraints; however, you can usually control other factors that make your document as pleasing to the reader as possible. Thus, as you construct your document, focus on the following categories:

- visual presentation
- proofreading and other nuances of presentation

VISUAL PRESENTATION[6]

All of us have been assigned to read something that we just dreaded to read. Why the dread? It's likely that we opened a page and saw something that tipped us off that the reading would be onerous. Maybe it was the font size; maybe it was the font itself; maybe we saw no break at all in the text for the first 20 pages.

Now the roles are reversed. You are the writer, and your job is to make sure that you do not prepare a document that your reader will dread wading through or might not read at all. Irrespective of your content (which one would hope is exceptional!), you can ensure that the reader picks up your document with anticipation and not dread.

---

[6] For a more expansive discussion of visuals in legal writing, see Ruth Anne Robins, *Painting with Print: Incorporating Concepts of Typographic and Layout Design into the Text of Legal Writing Documents*, 2 J. ALWD 108 (2004).

SOLUTIONS

1. Adjust **paragraph length** so that paragraphs are not too long. Likewise, make sure that paragraphs are not all too short.

Although there is no cardinal rule for how long a paragraph should be, once you get beyond four or five sentences, you are probably giving the reader too much information to take in all at once. Remember, readers of the English language take their cues from the indentations of new paragraphs. We see a line indented, and we start reprocessing the "new" subject. If there is too much information before the shift in paragraph, then the information can become garbled.

Similarly, no rule says that you are not allowed to write short, even one-sentence paragraphs. However, in legal writing, there is rarely anything substantive that does not require a multi-step process to explain.

Remember, we're talking about visuals here. Thus, if your paragraph *appears* too lengthy visually, it might be problematic. In general, you should see two or three indents on a page, or perhaps two indents and the continuation of a paragraph from the previous page. Again, this visual check is not a rule, but it is a good way to get a feel for how the reader will react to your document even before beginning to read.

2. Break paragraphs at logical points.

Each person entering law school has a different writing style. Some people write very short, choppy sentences, and some people write very lengthy and eloquent sentences. Each will have to make some accommodations to writing style, or at least learn to vary sentence length so that reading the document does not become monotonous.

There are various "logical" break points when you write legal documents. For instance, when writing about the specifics of a case (where the writer is including the holding, facts, and complete rationale of a case), you should break the paragraph between the facts and the rationale. When applying legal rules to a factual situation in an exam situation, you should break the paragraph between the legal definition and the application of that definition to the facts that you are discussing. When writing a statement of facts, your logical break point should come between the "story" you are telling and the current state of the legal procedure, e.g., "The client has since been arrested and has hired our firm to defend her against the charges." The logical breaking points help ensure that your organization directs the reader to understand your substance.

3. Be attentive to **symmetry.**

We are all terrorized, at some point, by the demand from an English teacher that our outlines required perfect symmetry. That is, if we had a "1" we needed a number "2," and if we had "a," "b," and "c" under number "1," then we needed the same for number "2." Those types of rules were rather draconian; however, the concept of a basic symmetry in your document is one that you should take into account.

Think about it. If you have a number "1" but not a number "2," doesn't that just mean that you have only one major thing to say and need nothing more than a good topic sentence to introduce your whole concept? The same holds true if you have an "a" but no "b." As you read the draft of your paper, take a look at subheadings that might be transformed into topic sentences.

The symmetry of a paper is relevant in other ways. Essentially, legal documents have two major components: the definitions, and how the definitions are applied to whatever facts you are analyzing. For the most part, those components of your document (whether an exam or a memorandum of law) should be relatively equal. Thus, once you've written your paper, eyeball it for its symmetry—both its visual symmetry (e.g., do you have one subheading that is inordinately longer than another?), and its substantive symmetry (e.g., do you have enough law in relation to the law that you're applying or enough application in relation to the law that you've defined?).

4. Add **white space** throughout the document.

A hurdle to readers understanding your substance is the initial feeling that they will be overwhelmed by the material. Alleviate this initial apprehension by adding space wherever possible.

White space acts to give the reader a breath—a chance to pause and regroup. The indentation of a paragraph helps, as does space between lines, or setting off single-spaced text (like lengthy quotations or issue statements) with a space before and after the single-spaced material. White space may also allow the readers to regroup when they begin to read a new segment of your paper. Thus, wherever possible, try not to begin a new segment of your paper at the bottom of your page but rather at the top of the next page.

Keep in mind, however, that you must follow the conventions of either your professors or a court. Ordinarily, legal documents are double-spaced (except for some material such as issue statements, headings, and lengthy quotations); thus, although you might think it looks more visually appealing to single-space all of your paragraphs but double-space between them, you might find that this type of format is not allowed.

As always, remember your audience.

5. Avoid **annoying fonts and methods of emphasis in text.** For the most part, professors and courts will guide you about the font and spacing you should be using. Adhere to those instructions. Don't think that we won't notice that you've changed your typeface to 9 and your line-spacing to 1.5 to ensure that your paper does not go beyond the allotted 10 pages. Many of us are getting older, and we simply won't be able to see what you've typed.

   Follow the guidelines concerning overall typeface and spacing. Consider this "creative" visual:

> *Memorandum of Law*
>
> TO: Professors LeClercq and Mika
> FROM: Student 1234
> Date: September 12, 2015
> Re: *Garibaldi v. Newsome*—analysis of Ohio Dog Bite Statute

Pretty, perhaps, but surely it did not follow a guideline. Even if readers try to ignore the heading, they will continuously wonder, "Why?" Now consider the next mishmash of a visual:

> The decision in Garrison demonstrates **EXACTLY** why the plaintiff has stated **a valid cause of action**! In Garrison, the court ruled that the plaintiff was due compensation for a dog bite ***even though the court ruled that the plaintiff provoked the dog!*** **HERE, THE PLAINTIFF, MR. GARIBALDI, DID NOTHING MORE THAN WALK BY THE DEFENDANT'S FENCE. HE SHOULD THEREFORE BE ENTITLED TO DAMAGES UNDER THE DOG BITE STATUTE!!!!!**

Notice how the manipulation of font and use of exclamation points manipulates the reader's reaction to the text. Here it reads as if the writer were SCREAMING at us. A bit of a useful tactic at times, but, misused or overused, the manipulation annoys readers and takes their concentration away from your discussion.

Try to use boldface sparingly, and avoid typing segments (except issue statements and questions presented) in all capital letters.

6. Watch **alignment.**

Being attentive to alignment is a crossover between watching symmetry and proofreading carefully.

Your professor or a court may require that various components of your writing be in a certain format. For instance, issues are typically single-spaced and block-indented or fully justified. Lengthy quotes are required to be single-spaced and fully justified.

Whether you are following a rule or merely attempting to ensure that your document is visually appealing, try to align the similar components uniformly and consistently. That is, if you are indenting your paragraphs by five spaces, make sure that each one is indented by five spaces. If you are block-indenting issue statements and you have more than one, make sure each is uniformly block-indented. If you have allowed for an extra line of space between an issue statement and the beginning of a paragraph in one section, make sure that you have similar spacing in any additional segments of the paper that you may have.

Although double-checking all of these features may seem tedious, doing so demonstrates that you are careful. This careful attention to detail will give you more credibility when the reader reflects on the substance of your document.

Compare these examples:

Example 1a. Memorandum of Law Segment

Inconsistent with other heading ▸	Issue:
Indented, rather than full block indent ▸	Whether an attorney commits malpractice when he cites a case that has been overturned and this results in an adverse decision in litigation against his client.
Not centered; Inconsistent with previous heading ▸	Facts
No indent, flush left ▸	Our client, Lima, Inc., an importer of limes, was represented by Joshen Gerardi in a litigation matter. In his brief, Gerardi relied heavily on a case that, unknown to him, the Texas Supreme Court had overturned six months before Lima's scheduled hearing. Our firm has been retained to bring a malpractice action against Gerardi.

All caps. Period after heading. Not separated from text or aligned with other headings ►

DISCUSSION. Lima's malpractice claim against Gerardi hinges on the legal issue of negligence, particularly the extent of Gerardi's duty to research the law properly and the breach of this duty. In Texas, a malpractice claim is based on the law of negligence. Cosgrove v. Grimes, 774 S.W.2d 662, 664 (Tex. 1989). To show that Gerardi was negligent, Lima must show that Gerardi had a duty to Lima, that he breached it, and that his breach was the proximate cause of Lima's harm. Id. at 665. An attorney has a duty to properly research the law and breaches this duty when he fails to do so. Morrill v. Graham, 27 Tex. 646, 651 (1864); Walder v. Texas, 85 S.W.3d 824, 827 (Tex. App. Waco 2002). Because Gerardi failed to discover pertinent case law in the case involving Lima and because this resulted in an adverse decision, it is likely a court will find Gerardi to be liable for malpractice.

Example 1b. Memorandum of Law Segment

Centered heading ►

ISSUE

Justified, bold, all-cap issue (often, but not always favored in law school) ►

WHETHER AN ATTORNEY COMMITS MALPRACTICE WHEN HE CITES A CASE THAT HAS BEEN OVERTURNED AND THIS RESULTS IN AN ADVERSE DECISION IN LITIGATION AGAINST HIS CLIENT.

Heading aligned with previous heading, all-cap, bold ►

FACTS

Our client, Lima, Inc., an importer of limes, was represented by Joshen Gerardi in a litigation matter.

In his brief, Gerardi relied heavily on a case that, unknown to him, the Texas Supreme Court had overturned six months before Lima's scheduled hearing. Our firm has been retained to bring a malpractice action against Gerardi.

Heading again aligned, all-cap, bold ►

DISCUSSION

Lima's malpractice claim against Gerardi hinges on the legal issue of negligence, particularly the extent of Gerardi's duty to research the law properly and the breach of this duty. In Texas, a malpractice claim is based on the law of negligence. Cosgrove v. Grimes, 774 S.W.2d 662, 664 (Tex. 1989). To show

> that Gerardi was negligent, Lima must show that Gerardi had a duty to Lima, that he breached it, and that his breach was the proximate cause of Lima's harm. Id. at 665. An attorney has a duty to properly research the law and breaches this duty when he fails to do so. Morrill v. Graham, 27 Tex. 646, 651 (1864); Walder v. Texas, 85 S.W.3d 824, 827 (Tex. App. Waco 2002). Because Gerardi failed to discover pertinent case law in the case involving Lima and because this resulted in an adverse decision, it is likely a court will find Gerardi to be liable for malpractice.

In **Example 1b**, readers can easily track the major headings and anticipate the material's content following them.

Let's consider another set of examples:

Example 2a. Law student cover letter

> Fredrick Youngdale III
> 111 Greenberg Drive
> Youngdale, Florida 33315
> 954-874-4598
> fyoungd&commat@aol.com
>
> September 16, 2015
>
> Ms. Shasheila Moore
> Hiring Partner
> Bracewell & Guiliani
> 1100 Pennzoil Place
> Houston, Texas 77002
>
> Dear Ms. Moore,
>
> Your firm uses second-year law students during the summer. I am applying for that position. I would like to visit your office for an interview when I will be in Houston, Nov. 16-19. Please let me know which day and what time would fit into your busy schedule. I am currently a second-year law student at the University of FarWest Florida. Still, Texas calls. I am currently taking Trial Advocacy and will participate in a mock trial later this fall. As you can tell, I am interested in trial work. Does your firm

Poor spacing in address. No "Re:" to apprise the reader the purpose of the letter ►

Weak introduction, disorganized; reflects a presumptuous attitude ►

One solid block of information; typos ►

offer trail experience to summer clerks? These and other questions I hope to have answered in our interview in November. Last summer I worked at my father's firm for six weeks, Youngdale & Youngdale of Miami. I drafted documents, and assisted the younger associate's as they prepared for big trials. As you can see, I have some legal experience and am eager for more.

Buried skills, experiences

Sincerely,

Fredrick Youngdale III

Example 2b. Law student cover letter

Fredrick Youngdale III
111 Greenberg Drive
Youngdale, Florida 33315
954-874-4598
fyoungd&commat@aol.com

September 16, 2015

Ms. Shasheila Moore
Hiring Partner
Bracewell & Guiliani
1100 Pennzoil Place
Houston, Texas 77002

Up-front statement of purpose ►

Re: Summer internship

Dear Ms. Moore,

Introduction acknowledges where applicant learned of job opening ►

reference to specific interest ►

Your August advertisement in *Florida Lawyer* caught my interest. Beti Lakshmi, a second-year associate at Bracewell & Guiliani in Dallas, recommended that I contact you because your firm focuses on trial work. As a second-year student at FarWest Florida School of Law, I have a strong, demonstrated interest in trial work, as evidenced by my participation this fall in an elective moot court. I would welcome the opportunity to work for your firm as a summer clerk.

Shows interest in firm—not merely a form letter ►	In the course of researching Bracewell & Guiliani, I discovered that you firm frequently represents clients who are involved in disputes with the DEA and INS over the seizure of their boats.
Here, <u>alignment</u> of skills and experience ►	• I grew up around boats. • Last summer I worked on admiralty questions at Youngdale & Youngdale as a summer associate.
<u>repetition</u> of bullet dots; <u>contrast</u> of list to body of text; <u>white space</u> ►	• This year I am enrolled in Admiralty Law. • I plan to focus on Admiralty Law when I graduate.
short paragraphs, appropriate politeness ►	I would like to visit your office for an interview when I will be in Houston, November 16-19. I hope to meet with you or someone in your office. I will contact you within the next two weeks and, if possible, arrange a time to meet that would be convenient. If you prefer, you can contact me at the number or email the address above. Thank you for your consideration. Sincerely, Frederick Youngdale III Enclosure Cc: Jacklyn Qadmi, Recruiting Coordinator

Note how the visuals of organization not only increase the reader's desire to read the letter, but also help group information. This adherence to the concept behind visuals for presentation will help the reader properly absorb the substance of Mr. Youngdale's request.

PROOFREADING AND OTHER NUANCES OF PRESENTATION

The last step of composing any written document is proofreading. By proofreading we mean examining every aspect of your document from organization, to word choice, to the visual presentation, to making sure that your professor's name is spelled correctly, to investigating that your font and line-spacing don't mysteriously change in the middle of a document; we don't mean just running spell check and glancing over your document. Checking presentation also means looking at the tiniest detail, such as a missing or stray comma, or whether something accidentally got italicized when it should not have been.

Using word processors to write our documents should, in theory, enable us to write better documents. We can now cut and paste material to shift substance when we edit, and we can cut and paste direct quotes or citations from other documents. We can also use spell check to let us know if we have misspelled the obvious. However, rely too much on the word processor for correcting our spelling, and we forget that the word processor did not necessarily know the intended word. (Many an attorney and student has been embarrassed by the inclusion of the terms "pubic policy," "state statues," and "Untied States of America.") We also do not always remember that when we cut and paste, we are often cutting and pasting a different font from a source document. The careful individual makes sure that the incorporated font is uniform. Any of these oversights will distract the reader.

SOLUTIONS

Rather than enumerate solutions, we thought the better plan was to enumerate "annoyances"—things that annoy professors and courts.

1. **Misspellings.** We all make mistakes, but a document that is laden with misspellings indicates that the writer is either very sloppy or did not take the time to proofread. Generally, a writer who is unable to take the time to proofread is regarded as one who will also not take the time to do a good job with the legal substance. Misspellings are more egregious when it seems as though the person did not even take the time to use spell check. Although spell check is not the cure-all for spelling errors, it is a first step in ensuring that obvious spelling errors will be caught.

   The misspelling of key legal terms such as plaintiff or defendant appears careless, and spelling the names of the parties incorrectly conveys to the reader that you don't care enough to spell the names right. Unless you set your word processor properly, spell check will not pick up errors in segments that are typed in all capital letters, and sometimes not in headings and subheadings either. Thus, even if you use spell check, it will not flag errors in your issue statements. Many a student has been embarrassed by turning in a paper with four or five typographical errors left in an issue statement that the student assumed were corrected by spell check!

2. **Varying** names/party positions throughout a document. There is little more distracting in a document than changing the spelling of names throughout the document. The writer identifies a party as one name, then switches to a variation of that name, then switches back to the original name. Rather than focusing on what you're saying about the case, the

reader may be thinking, "Hmmm, I thought the defendant was named Johansen, but then maybe it's Johnson?" The same distraction can happen when dealing with case names.

A similar distraction is switched party positions (e.g., the defendant suddenly becomes the plaintiff and then back again a few pages later). Make sure you proofread to ensure you are consistent.

3. **Misusing apostrophes.** Remember that, except for "its," possessives have apostrophes and plurals do not. An apostrophe, like any other punctuation mark, is a cue to the reader. Thus, if the reader sees "plaintiffs," the reader will assume there are multiple plaintiffs. If the writer intended to say, "Plaintiff's vehicle," the reader will become distracted and will likely have to re-read the sentence to understand the proper context. This forced re-reading, again, defeats your purpose of writing a fluid and easy-to-follow document.

   It's easy to make mistakes with apostrophes. Your mind might have been working faster than your typing fingers, or maybe you were just thinking of something else at the time. But trouble with apostrophes is one of the major pet peeves of professors and judges, so make sure that you carefully proofread all of your plurals and possessives. (See also Chapter 4, Punctuating with Style.)

4. **Cutting and pasting.** Problems can occur when you cut and paste a section or citation from another document without matching the font or line spacing. Although it may seem easy to "lift" a properly formatted citation from a computerized source, keep in mind that the citation may not be properly formatted font-wise. Sometimes citations in other sources are completely underlined or completely italicized—both unacceptable for documents turned in for your writing classes. The text itself may be a different size from the document that you are constructing.

   Make sure that any material cut and pasted from another document is uniform with the remainder of the document that you are working on. This includes quotation marks that might appear differently from font to font.

   A second cutting-and-pasting problem occurs when the student cuts and pastes material from a sample the professor provides. Quite often, your writing professor gives you samples to make your life easier, but if you're using these samples as the basis for your own document, modify the additions as necessary. Again, it is embarrassing for the student when the first thing that the professor discovers is that the student has not bothered to change material from the sample, including the name of the court, the judge, or even the parties. When you incorporate samples, make sure that they reflect the *current* assignment.

   Also, be careful before pasting language your professor might have included in a critiqued draft returned to you electronically. The suggested language may not make sense if you make other revisions to the paper that might eliminate the need for the suggested wording. Thus, whenever a professor suggests wording, the student should look at it critically and decide whether that wording or some modification makes sense within the context of the paper.

Anything that is cut and pasted together should be proofread to make sure that the document does not appear to be cut and pasted together.

5. **Nuances.** The concept of paying attention to nuances has been implicit in almost everything we have written so far. Time and time again, we have repeated that various writers' oversights can distract a reader from the substance. Some are very obvious, and some are subtle distractions. Try to pick up on what those distractions might be and correct them.

   Paying attention to these nuances makes a visually pleasing document, and it indicates to the reader that you took the time to pay attention to detail. That care and attention are important to your success in law school—and your success as an attorney.

What to Remember

- **Adjust paragraph length** so that paragraphs are not too lengthy or too short.
- Add **white space** where possible.
- Review your document so that **spacing, text alignment, and font size is consistent.**
- **Proofread** and **correct spelling errors** or spelling inconsistencies.
- Be **attentive to apostrophes** to ensure they are being properly used.
- Be careful about **cutting and pasting text**.
- Make sure **font is consistent** and that your text does not use mixed fonts or word emphasis that distract the reader.
- Pay attention to **nuances**—revise anything that you think may distract the reader.

The Daily News

Eleanor Roosevelt Receives Impressive Plague for her Humanitarian Efforts

ANSWERS

CHAPTER 1: REVIEWING THE BASICS

Answers to Higher Competency Quiz

1. **Parallelism.** Mr. Helm, seeking to overturn his sentence, **sued** the state, saying it violated the Eighteenth Amendment's prohibition against "cruel and unusual punishment" with the no-parole add-on to his life sentence, and **failed** to apply any proportionality test. (You might also divide the sentence into two sentences.)

2. **Word choice.** "Prison for life" is different **from** "prison for life without parole."

3. **Reflexive/objective pronoun.** He asked his attorneys to "please send the history of earlier cases to my wife and **me**" so the two could help the team with the research.

4. **Compound adjective/adjective.** All the cases and the anecdotes over **10 years old** were not helpful.

5. **Ambiguous passive.** Attorneys acknowledged that Helm had a fraudulent check for $100 that **he** cashed at the grocery store.

6. **Word choice. Because** Helm had been arrested for three drunk driving offenses, the system had already labeled him a recidivist.

7. **Misplaced modifier.** One question was whether this history was **for only** "relatively 'minor' crimes."

8. **Essential/nonessential phrase.** The court looked at three objective criteria **that** it enumerated in the opinion for the first time.

9. **Comma splice.** Mr. Helm had a great deal at stake. He had quit drinking and had made a mistake with the check. (Writers could also use a semicolon, or a comma and simple conjunction.)

10. **Compound adjective before a noun.** In 1995, the Supreme Court narrowed the earlier **proportionality-guarantee** principle with five more principles to use in cases of life without parole.

CHAPTER 2: CREATING SENTENCES WITH STYLE

Answers to Exercise 1. Unraveling Tough Sentences; Creating and Connecting Sentences with Style

1. **Lengthy, separation of subject/verb.** The **district court concluded** that the expert testimony should not have been admitted**. In reaching** this conclusion, **the court noted** that the expert witness was not qualified to be testifying about rocket fuel. **The court also noted** that the flash point of rocket fuel was irrelevant given that the suit was an action for battery.

2. **Separation subject/verb, too much information in a sentence.** The **judge recused** himself from the case after he revealed that he had gone to high school with the plaintiff's attorney. **He also acknowledged** that his children went to the same school as the plaintiff's children.

3. **Front-loaded sentence, interruptions.** If the prosecution suppresses evidence favorable to the accused, **that suppression** may violate due process. **This violation** occurs if the favorable evidence is material to either guilt or punishment. It does not matter whether this suppression was in good or bad faith.

4. **Lengthy, separation subject/verb, interrupted.** In the majority opinion, the **Chief Justice wrote** that the confession should have been suppressed. **The Justice noted** that the defendant had requested counsel when he was first placed in a police car and had repeated his request while in a holding cell. **The Justice further noted** that the defendant had confessed only when told that his attorney would be delayed by a few hours.

5. Two of the judges questioned the **procedural problem** with the case.

The **procedural problem** was that the attorney had mislabeled the motion.

6. The plaintiff's allegation was that she was a victim of **intentional infliction of emotional distress.** Proving **intentional infliction of emotional distress** requires that a plaintiff demonstrate that the defendant engaged in purposely malicious behavior that goes "beyond the decency of the norms of a polite society."

7. In a law-student newsletter, a third-year **student plagiarized** the writing of a nationally syndicated columnist.

8. The **Federalist Society discovered** the plagiarism.

Answers to Exercise 2. Avoiding Error

1. Dangling element. After researching both primary and secondary sources, the editorial **board reviews** the law review drafts. (You might also want to flip-flop the elements of the sentence.)

2. Misplaced modifier (and verb split by comma)**.** The court **reversed only** the conviction for **murder but** sustained the conviction for breaking and entering.

3. Ambiguous pronouns. The client **asked his attorney** whether he had to tell the attorney the complete truth and whether **not telling him the truth** would affect their relationship.

4. Ambiguous pronoun. While the client was speaking, the attorney seemed to develop a headache as well as have fears about taking the case, so the client had to find a way to ameliorate **the fears of the attorney** before he could reveal a few more facts of his story.

5. Parallelism. When arguing before the court, new attorneys must remember:

a. to dress appropriately;
b. to address the court directly;
c. **to treat** all members of the staff with courtesy; and
d. **to follow** strict time limitations.

6. Parallelism. A patient may have a cause of action against a doctor if the doctor examined him, determined that he was an appropriate candidate for an experimental treatment, made hospital arrangements, but, in the haste of the consultation, **did not inform** the patient of the risk associated with this experimental treatment.

Answers to Exercise 3. Incorporating Authority

1. **Case name as subject of sentence. In** *United States v. Frost*, 125 F.3d 346 (6th Cir. 1997), the court originally set forth the test for proving the cause of action against the defendants.

2. **Lack of transitions between citations.** The Supreme Court made its decision regarding suppressing favorable evidence in *Brady v. Maryland*, 373 U.S. 83 (1963). **Later**, in *Kyles v. Whitley*, 514 U.S. 419 (1995), the Court reviewed the materiality requirement and held that a "touchstone of materiality is a reasonable probability of a different result."

3. **Quotation may be paraphrased.** The court held that an individual does not waive his/her right to privacy in all instances, but rather that a waiver of privacy rights in one situation does not mean privacy has been waived in another situation. [cite]

4. **Unnecessary direct quotation except for distinguishing language.** The court acknowledged that a legal search of someone who has been stopped by police is assessed in part by looking at the "**reason and experience**" of the police officer who made the stop. [cite]

CHAPTER 3: CHOOSING WORDS WITH STYLE

Answers to Concluding Exercise

1. He hired an outside company **to investigate** finances.

2. The judge **said** he had never seen such blatant plagiarism.

3. **Fred** Fender **denied the** charge, **saying he** had been unfairly persecuted for his secretary's errors.

4. **The clerk worked late** to investigate the two, similar filings.

5. The next morning, the **clerk presented** the answer that fully reinforced the ACLU's research.

6. **Jargon.** This dishonesty reflected on the veracity of any lawyer and on the court.

7. **Dangling Element.** After looking for other similar cases, the judge discovered several instances of plagiarism in other jurisdictions that the courts had dealt with publicly.

8. **Ambiguous pronoun.** The judge found for the ACLU and ordered a strict scrutiny of all of Fender's firm's documents. **This decision** was followed by a public reprimand.

9. The managing partner had to **ensure** that the firm was safe from any criticism from the legal community.

10. The firm had **continual** CLE classes on ethics.

CHAPTER 4: PUNCTUATING WITH STYLE

Answers to Concluding Exercise

1. **Punctuation compound adjective.** In Dallas a 16-year-old kid with a glossy-red convertible was stopped for speeding.

2. **Fragment after period.** He pulled over to the side of the **road and** was so nervous he hit the curb.

3. **Punctuation around quotation marks.** "Ohmygodno," the policeman heard him chanting.

4. **Fragment after semicolon.** "This will be an easy stop," the policeman said into his car speaker, "because he is already admitting he's in trouble."

5. **Punctuation with series and internal comma.** First the policeman walked completely around the car, noting its condition; stopped by the passenger window; and asked to see the boy's driver's license.

6. **Colon introduces list.** He asked for information: the driver's name, owner of the vehicle, where the driver was going, and if he knew he was exceeding the speed limit.

7. **Unnecessary indentation for short quotation.** The police officer said, "You have the right to refuse to answer these simple questions, but I advise you to answer them and clear up any confusion now."

8. **Punctuation introductory clause; separation of subject and verb with comma.** When the boy quickly spouted the answers, the police officer wrote several of them down and grunted at the rest.

9. **Essential/nonessential clause.** The process needed to go quickly, **which** the officer knew from experience.

10. **Punctuation between two complete sentences.** Some speeders will become indignant and argumentative, **and** some will be embarrassed and just want to sign the forms and leave.

CHAPTER 5: ORGANIZING WITH STYLE

Answers to Concluding Exercise

1. **The paragraph's logic is incorrect.** The structure of the paragraph should follow the format of "general rule, elaborations to the general rule, application of the law to the facts, and the prediction for litigation." A possible revision:

    In California, a person who chooses what is considered an offensive combination of letters for a personalized license plate may be denied the opportunity to have that plate. Courts have interpreted a combination of letters as offensive if they have a sexual connotation, if they suggest a derogatory meaning, or if they are insulting to a certain segment of the population. The standard used to assess offensiveness is the "reasonable person who understands the language [being used]." The non-offensive intent of the person using the phrase/letters in question is irrelevant. Because the letters "FU" are commonly understood as shorthand for a sexual phrase, it is likely that a court would find the plaintiff's requested plate offensive. It is irrelevant that the plaintiff did not intend to convey a derogatory meaning. As a result, it is likely that the plaintiff will be denied the right to have the ILVTOFU license plate.

2. **The headings should correspond** to the legal elements that are set out in an introductory paragraph that identifies the rule of law being applied. The headings should also combine the applicable facts to the rule of law to explain why an element of the legal test has been met. Effective headings might be:

    1. The wearing of the Hillary Clinton shirt might not be considered protected speech because there was not a great likelihood that the message would be understood.
    2. The wearing of the Hillary Clinton shirt might not be considered protected speech because an objective observer might not have understood the message.
    3. Even if the wearing of the t-shirt is considered protected speech, the school was likely within its rights to ask the plaintiff to turn the shirt inside out because of previous disruptions that had occurred at the

school when others wore celebrity t-shirts.

3. **The headings must reflect the text and must be parallel.** Better headings would be:

    1. The dog is unlikely to be considered well-trained because the records do not establish sufficient reliability.
    2. The dog is unlikely to be considered sufficiently reliable because she did not do well in certification training.
    3. The dog is unlikely to be considered sufficiently reliable because she had many false positives after she was certified.

4. **Adding a topic sentence and transition will help the reader follow your content.** Possible revision:

    The court examined various factors in determining whether a search was justified. First, the court determined that a police officer could conduct a search only if it was reasonably believed that the defendant was carrying contraband. **Second,** the court determined that a stop could be made if the police officer believed a defendant looked suspicious. **In determining what was regarded as suspicious,** the court **stated** that an officer could look at various factors, including whether the neighborhood was generally crime-ridden whether the defendant looked out-of-place or was attempting to evade police.

5. **Generally, verb tenses for setting out what occurred in a previously decided case are written in past tense.** Here is a possible revision:

    In general, the law **is** that the First Amendment protects freedom of speech and expression. In the Supreme Court case of *Tinker*, the Court **considered** whether wearing black armbands (to protest the Vietnam War) **was** protected in a school. In reaching its decision, the Court concluded that the school **had** the right to restrict some forms of personal expression, but not the wearing of the armbands. The Court further **stated** that, prior to restricting expression, the school **failed** to present evidence that the restricted expression might have caused unrest.

INDEX

Made in the USA
Monee, IL
05 November 2026

67385921R00074